ARTISTIK LONDON

Written by
Simon Cropper

Illustrated by
Alain Bouldouyre

AUTHENTIK BOOKS

Les Editions du Mont-Tonnerre
4 bis Villa du Mont-Tonnerre
Paris XVe arrondissement

AUTHENTIK ®

Published by The Globe Pequot Press
246 Goose Lane, P.O. Box 480
Guilford, Connecticut 06437
www.globepequot.com

© 2007 Authentik Books
www.authentikbooks.com

Produced in France by Les Editions du Mont-Tonnerre
Text and illustrations copyright © Wilfried LeCarpentier

Authentik® Trademark, Wilfried LeCarpentier
4 bis Villa du Mont-Tonnerre, Paris XVe arrondissement
www.monttonnerre.com

ISBN 978-0-7627-4636-1
First Edition

Printed and bound in China

LES EDITIONS DU MONT-TONNERRE
Founder and Publisher: Wilfried LeCarpentier
Editor at Large: William Landmark
Managing Editor: Caroline Favreau

AUTHENTIK ARTISTIK LONDON
Restaurants, Wine and Food Consultant: Gérard Poirot
Project Editor: Nicola Mitchell
Project Editor: Jessica Fortescue
Copy Editor: Helen Stuart, Carly Jane Lock, Sandra Iskander
Proofreader: Natasha Edwards
Researcher: Jessica Phelan
Editorial Assistant: Jennifer Parker

Creative Director: Lorenzo Locarno
Artistic Director: Nicolas Mamet
Graphic Designer: Amélie Dommange
Layout Artist: Marie-Thérèse Gomez
Cover Design and Packaging: Nicolas Mamet
Cartographer: Map Resources
Map Illustrator: Kouakou
Pre-Press and Production: Studio Graph'M, Paris

GLOBE PEQUOT PRESS
President and Publisher: Scott Watrous
Editorial Director: Karen Cure

ACKNOWLEDGEMENTS

Special thanks to Marie-Christine Levet, Scott Watrous, Karen Cure,
Gunnar Stenmar, Gérard Paulin, Pierre Jovanovic, Jacques Derey,
Bruno de sa Moreira and Yuko Oso, Francesco Betti, Charles Walker

Uncover the Exceptional

The Authentik book collection was born out of a desire to explore beauty and craftsmanship in every domain and in whatever price bracket. The books describe the aesthetic essence of a city, homing in on modern-day artisans who strive for perfection and whose approach to their work is as much spiritual as commercial. Written by specialist authors, the guides delve deep into the heart of a capital and, as a result, are excellent companions for both locals and nomadic lovers of fine living. Their neat size, made to fit into a suit or back pocket, make them easy and discreet to consult, and their elegant design and insider selection of addresses will ensure that you get to the heart of the local scene and blend in perfectly with it. There is even a notebook at the back for some cerebral scribbling of your own. In all, Authentik Books are the perfect accessory for uncovering the exceptional, whether in the arts, fashion, design or gastronomy.

Wilfried LeCarpentier
Founder and Publisher

Victoria & Albert Museum
Cromwell Road, SW7

Contents

How to Use This Guide

Ever felt like jumping in a black cab at Heathrow airport and saying, "Take me to the centre of things!"? Well, this book does the work of a very knowledgeable cabbie.

Artistik London consists of ten chapters of insider information on the capital's thriving arts scene. Besides highlighting the unmissable mainstream destinations, the guide ventures into little known insider territory: the open studios, the small but influential galleries and edgy performance spaces. There's even information on where to study should you decide to stay in the city and feed the artist in you.

The directory at the end of each chapter gives the addresses of the places mentioned, plus the details of other essential stops too numerous to include in the chapter. The maps at the back of the guide cover the principal streets of central London. Use the map references added to the addresses to find the general location of our listings.

The guide online

Using the **2D BAR CODE** below you can load all the addresses onto a mobile phone with Internet access. This unique aspect of the book enables you to travel extra light.

scan here

How to access content on your mobile phone

If your mobile phone has Internet access and a built-in camera go to

www.scanlife.com

Download the free software that allows your mobile phone to identify the bar code. Downloading takes less than one minute. Then go to your personal file icon which will appear on your phone's menu screen, and select the icon **Scanlife**. Next, point your camera at the 2D bar code. A sound confirms that the bar code has been recognized. You can then access the directories on your phone.

A MIGHTY
CREATIVE CAULDRON

Swiss Re Tower ('Gherkin')
30 St Mary Axe, EC3

Previous page: Aldwych Theatre
Aldwych, WC2

Leabharlanna Fhine Gall

How things have changed. Barely two or three decades ago, mention of 'the average Londoner' called to mind a phlegmatic sort of character, a creature of habit and rueful humour, at ease in the assumed superiority of the British Isles and irredeemably insular. A person more interested in 'the dogs' than the arts. Today, if there is indeed such a thing as an average Londoner, he or she is something very different: connected, nomadic, contradictory and curious. London has become one of the most conspicuously multicultural cities in the world, and into this colossal cauldron are pitched people and art from every corner of the globe.

There's no doubt about it, these are exciting times. London's artistic outlets have never been so numerous, nor so varied, nor so fit for purpose. **Tate Modern** has been a roaring success since it opened in 2000, and major expansion plans are underway. The celebrated **Saatchi Gallery** has moved to larger, supremely prestigious premises in Chelsea. Beneficiaries of extensive renovation programmes in the last few years include polymath powerhouse the **Barbican**, the **Whitechapel Arts Gallery**, the **Wigmore Hall** and the **Coliseum**.

Sadler's Wells
Rosebery Avenue, EC1

Meanwhile, the South Bank arts complex has been given what the *Guardian* calls "a thrilling but subtle makeover".

There's exciting new architecture, too, not only from established stars like Norman Foster and Richard Rogers, but from rising talents like Will Alsop, whose wonky-legged **Peckham Library** elevated him to Stirling Prize winner status. There are landmarks like the **Swiss Re** tower and the **London Eye** as well as street art, including anarchic rats and kissing policemen by wittily subversive graffiti artist Banksy.

There are the festivals that bring a concentrated barrage of the world's finest to London from the **Proms** to **Dance Umbrella** via the **London Film Festival** and the **Frieze Art Fair**. And, of course, there are the world famous museums and performance venues, which form a vital part of London's reputation and sense identity. Hallowed names like the **Royal Albert Hall**, the **Royal Opera House**, the **V&A**, the **National Gallery**, the **British Museum**, **Sadler's Wells**… the riches seem endless.

A significant proportion of the city's chroniclers argue that London is more important than New York these days. Even Michael Bloomberg, the Big Apple's mayor, has publicly acknowledged that London is poised to become the "capital of the world", and if he says so, there

Tate Modern
Bankside, SE1

must be truth in it. **Tate Modern** is reckoned by critics on both sides of the Atlantic as superior to the revamped Museum of Modern Art in New York, **Christie's** and **Sotheby's** continue to break art sale records and London rivals New York's position in the finance market. No wonder people are saying London has never had it so good.

Yet the capital's vivacious cultural scene didn't come about by chance. A lot of hard fighting has gone into achieving and maintaining the profile and funding the arts currently enjoy, and there's no shortage of professionals who think these levels of subsidy are too low.

But locals are not complaining, because there's never been more art in London than there is today and the choice is electrifying. Even the city's culinary scene has been transformed thanks to innovative restaurateurs.

Finding your way to the best of all this creative activity is not always easy, but by highlighting the capital's essential addresses in every major artistic discipline, this book aims to show you how.

BOOKISH PURSUITS
AND CITY SCRIBES

The Charles Dickens Museum
48 Doughty St, WC1

Previous page: Hatchards
187 Piccadilly, W1

Writing in London almost always becomes writing about London. The pursuit, through one channel or another, of compendious knowledge, unorthodox knowledge, the struggle to understand. 'Writing the city' was a London thing long before the phrase was coined. This huge hub of a global network, Sherlock Holmes' Dr Watson calls it a "great cesspool into which all the loungers of the Empire are irresistibly drained," has been a factory of material and writers since men first put quill to parchment.

Writers at home

Most of the UK's publishers have their headquarters in London, the city is the centre of British film and television production, and it has the country's greatest concentration of theatres, which gives plenty of employment to an author, whether a native Londoner like Chaucer or an out-of-towner like Shakespeare.

What's more, Britain's liberal attitudes have long made the city a safe haven for overseas writers on the run, the most illustrious being Voltaire. Others, like the great Japanese novelist **Natsume Soseki**, came to study the

English language or, like the French poets Stéphane Mallarmé, Arthur Rimbaud and Paul Verlaine, to teach a foreign one.

The slums described by Dickens have long gone, and the Thames estuary so evocatively conjured up at the start of **Joseph Conrad**'s *Heart of Darkness* is sailed by very different craft today, but the London homes of a long list of writers are still standing. Many are within easy walking distance of each other in the centre of the city and adorned with blue circular plaques as an aid for passersby. Bloomsbury, a district synonymous with literary excellence, is a good place to start.

The **Charles Dickens Museum** is the only one of the great author's London residences still in existence, he wrote *Oliver Twist* and *Nicholas Nickleby* here, and its four floors are packed with memorabilia: letters, manuscripts and his writing desk.

Keats House, in leafy Hampstead, was home to the Romantic poet John Keats from 1818-1820 where he wrote *Ode to a Nightingale* in the garden. It displays manuscripts, letters, prints, paintings and objects relating to his life and the Romantic movement and is a venue for poetry readings and literary events. Finally, the house of British historian and essayist **Thomas Carlyle**

is as much a snapshot of Victorian literary life as a memorial to one man, with creaky floorboards and the original fixtures and fittings.

The best bookstores

London has some wonderful bookshops. The cavernous **Foyles**, in business at the current address since 1906, is one of the most famous in the world, and was given a terrific major refurbishment in 2004. Gone are the eccentric days when books were arranged by publisher rather than by author or subject, its trading practices are now much the same as those you'll find anywhere else. Its huge stock contains works on 56 specialist subjects and a large music section. Foyles also has an active schedule of signing and reading event, and its famous literary luncheons, held since 1930, bring together famous writers and some 600 ticket holders. These days the meetings are held at the Dorchester or Grosvenor House hotels.

Hatchards on Piccadilly, supplier of reading matter to the Queen, is even more venerable, having been founded in 1797. The literary enclave feels like a gentleman's club, with its dark wood shelving and spiral staircase; former customers include Byron, former Prime Minister Benjamin Disraeli and Oscar Wilde. It holds regular signings and is renowned for its excellent selection of hardbacks and signed copies.

London Review Bookshop
14 Bury Place, WC1

The chain book stores **Borders** and **Waterstone's** carry rich arrays of authors and subjects, and new titles are often discounted or included in three-for-two promotions. The provision of cafés in many of their branches is another boon. For the biggest stock, go to **Waterstone's** on Gower Street or on Piccadilly, probably the largest bookshop in Europe.

Still, the best browsing and buying are invariably to be had in the smaller, more individual shops like **Daunt Books**, **Metropolitan Books** or **Primrose Hill Books**.

The relatively new **London Review Bookshop**, owned by the bi-monthly heavyweight literary journal *The London Review*, is small but enthusiastic, and it has some of the most stimulating stock anywhere in the city. A good range of literary magazines and its savvy and friendly staff, as well as frequent readings, talks and debates, add to its charms. Newer still is **Crockatt & Powell**, which runs a book club. **Blenheim Books** is another such independent, thriving on a personal approach to the bookseller's trade and operating out of a swish and welcoming shop in Notting Hill and a deeply groovy website.

Superior secondhand

The short pedestrian lane Cecil Court, which runs between Charing Cross Road and Saint Martin's Lane, offers particularly rich pickings for those in search of something secondhand. Two of the most notable booksellers here are **Marchpane**, which is strong on children's books, and **Nigel Williams Rare Books**, whose speciality is first editions of 20th-century titles, as well as detective fiction.

Antiques and collectibles

Places like **Bernard J. Shapero Rare Books**, **Biblion** and **Jarndyce** are excellent sources of antique and collectable volumes, all staffed by specialist booksellers and stocked with books that command prices anywhere

City literature

The Soho of **Chris Petit's** *Robinson*, the west London of **Martin Amis's** *London Fields* and the East End of **Monica Ali's** *Brick Lane* all look, sound and feel different – three squares of a patchwork Möbius strip.

Where these and other authors choose to zero in on a particular bit of urban terrain, **Peter Ackroyd** chooses to treat London as a character and relate its biography (*London: The Biography*).

But the writer and film maker **Iain Sinclair** treats London as a mesh of occult forces and currents, a city of ghosts and impulses at work behind the visible surfaces. Sinclair is the most eminent of the city's psychogeographers, the patient cartographer of unsuspected contours in novels like *White Chappell, Scarlet Tracings* and *Downriver*, and non-fiction books like *Lights Out for the Territory, London Orbital* and the thick collaborative tome of which he was editor, *London City of Disappearances*.

Also a prolific essayist, he's one of Britain's best living writers; he says "the inspiration of London comes from the argument between its multilayered past and its neurotic future: the impulse to erase memory and start again."

from £10 to tens of thousands. **Henry Sotheran** is older than many of its books, having been trading in London since the Battle of Waterloo. The focus here is on English literature, travel, natural history, art, and rare prints. **Simon Finch Rare Books**, on the other hand, is younger and dedicated to modern English and continental literature and the arts.

02

Brick Lane, E1

Writers at home

Thomas Carlyle
24 Cheyne Row, SW3
⊖ Sloane Square
☏ 020 7352 7087
nationaltrust.org.uk
⊕ 14/H17

Agatha Christie
58 Sheffield Terrace, W8
⊖ Notting Hill Gate
⊕ Off map

Joseph Conrad
17 Gillingham St, SW1
⊖ Victoria
⊕ 14/M14

Charles Dickens
48 Doughty St, WC1
⊖ Russell Square
☏ 020 7405 2127
dickensmuseum.com
⊕ 3/R5

T.S. Eliot
3 Kensington Court
Gdns, W8
⊖ High St Kensington
⊕ 9/E12

Ian Fleming
22 Ebury St, SW1
⊖ Victoria
⊕ 14/L14

Keats House
Keats Grove, NW3
⊖ Hampstead
☏ 020 7435 2062
cityoflondon.gov.uk
⊕ Off map

A.A. Milne
13 Mallord St, SW3
⊖ South Kensington
⊕ 13-14/G17

Percy Bysshe Shelley
15 Poland St, W1
⊖ Oxford Circus
⊕ 7/N8

Natsume Soseki
80b The Chase, SW4
⊖ Clapham Common
☏ 020 7720 8718
⊕ Off map

Oscar Wilde
34 Tite St, SW3
⊖ Sloane Square
⊕ 14/J16

Virginia Woolf
29 Fitzroy Sq, W1
⊖ Great Portland St
⊕ 7/N6

London writing now

The Literary London Journal
literarylondon.org

London Books
londonbooks.co.uk

London Libraries
londonlibraries.org

The best bookstores

Blackwell's
100 Charing Cross Rd,
WC2
⊖ Tottenham Court Rd
① 020 7292 5100
bookshop.blackwell
⊕ 7/P8

Blenheim Books
11 Blenheim Crescent,
W11
⊖ Ladbroke Grove
① 020 7792 0777
blenheimbooks.co.uk
⊕ 5/A8

Borders
203 Oxford St, W1
⊖ Oxford Circus
① 020 7292 1600
borders.co.uk
⊕ 6/K8

Crockatt & Powell
119 Lower Marsh St, SE1
⊖ Waterloo
① 020 7928 0234
crockattpowell.com
⊕ 11/S12

Daunt Books
83 Marylebone High St, W1
⊖ Baker Street
① 020 7224 2295
dauntbooks.co.uk
⊕ 6/L6

Foyles
113-119 Charing Cross
Rd, WC2
⊖ Tottenham Court Rd
① 020 7437 5660
foyles.co.uk
⊕ 7/P8

Hatchards
187 Piccadilly, W1
⊖ Piccadilly Circus
① 020 7439 9921
hatchards.co.uk
⊕ 11/O10

John Sandoe
10 Blacklands Terrace, SW3
⊖ Sloane Square
① 020 7589 9473
johnsandoe.com
⊕ 14/J15

**London Review
Bookshop**
14 Bury Pl, WC1
⊖ Holborn
① 020 7269 9030
lrbshop.co.uk
⊕ 7/Q7

02

Metropolitan Books
49 Exmouth Market, EC1
⊖ Angel
① 020 7278 6900
metropolitanbooks.co.uk
⊕ 4/T5

Primrose Hill Books
134 Regent's Park Rd, NW1
⊖ Chalk Farm
① 020 7586 2022
primrosehillbooks.co.uk
⊕ 2/K1

Waterstone's
82 Gower St, WC1
⊖ Euston Square
① 020 7636 1577
waterstones.com
⊕ 3/O5

Simon Finch Rare Books
53 Maddox St, W1

Superior secondhand

Henry Sotheran
2-5 Sackville St, W1
⊖ Green Park
Ⓒ 020 7439 6151
sotherans.co.uk
⊕ 11/N10

Marchpane
16 Cecil Court, WC2
⊖ Leicester Square
Ⓒ 020 7836 8661
marchpane.com
⊕ 7/P9

Nigel Williams Rare Books
25 Cecil Court, WC2
⊖ Leicester Square
Ⓒ 020 7836 7757
nigelwilliams.com
⊕ 7/P9

Quinto/Francis Edwards
48A Charing Cross Rd, WC2
⊖ Leicester Sq
Ⓒ 020 7379 7669
⊕ 7/P8

Skoob Books
Brunswick Centre, WC1
⊖ Russell Square
Ⓒ 020 7278 8760
skoob.com
⊕ 3/Q5

Ulysses
40 Museum St, WC1
⊖ Holborn
Ⓒ 020 7831 1600
⊕ 7/Q7

02

Antiques and collectibles

Bernard J. Shapero Rare Books
32 St George St, W1
⊖ Bond Street
Ⓒ 020 7493 0876
shapero.com
⊕ 6/M9

Biblion
1-7 Davies Mews, W1
⊖ Bond Street
Ⓒ 020 7629 1374
biblion.com
⊕ 6/L9

Gekoski
15a Bloomsbury Sq, WC1
⊖ Holborn
Ⓒ 020 7404 6676
⊕ 7/Q7

Jarndyce
46 Great Russell St, WC1
⊖ Tottenham Court Rd
Ⓒ 020 7631 4220
jarndyce.co.uk
⊕ 7/P7

Simon Finch Rare Books
53 Maddox St, W1
⊖ Oxford Circus
Ⓒ 020 7499 0974
simonfinch.com
⊕ 6/M9

Quaritch
8 Lower John St, W1
⊖ Piccadilly Circus
Ⓒ 020 7734 2983
quaritch.com
⊕ 6-7/N9

See page 9
to scan the
directory

MUSIC, THEATRE AND DANCE

Royal Albert Hall
Kensington Gore, SW7

Previous page: Wigmore Hall
36 Wigmore St, W1

Theatre, music and dance have ancient connections to the British capital and are in excellent shape today. Many of the main performance venues have been comprehensively renovated since 2000 and the rock-solid base of native talent is continually spiced up by collaborators from overseas. The cultural importance of the performing arts is recognized in a healthy flow of state subsidy and private sponsorship, and audiences are very open-minded and hungry for new fare. It all makes for an exciting and dynamic array of epic, intimate, crowd-pleasing or avant-garde events right across the city.

03

Classical music

London has an unbroken tradition of classical music-making, varying from Mozart, who composed his first symphony here in 1764, at 180 Ebury Street, to Handel and Vaughan Williams. Many of the country's principal orchestras such as the London Symphony Orchestra (whose home is the **Barbican Centre**, where it performs 90 concerts a year), the London Philharmonic Orchestra, the London Sinfonietta and the BBC Symphony Orchestra are based in the city.

What's more, very nearly every major international orchestra, conductor and soloist comes to London to perform at some time or other and a good number, such as Alfred Brendel and Mitsuko Uchida, live here.

Of the main performance venues, the Barbican Centre, already a leader for the quality of its programming, is better than ever thanks to a £30 million refit that greatly improved the acoustics of its main auditorium. Its Great Performers series brings in soloists and ensembles from all over the world, and mini festivals honour contemporary composers. Also renovated (at even greater cost) is the **Royal Festival Hall**, which reopened in summer 2007.

Newcomers include the airy and excellent-sounding auditorium at **Cadogan Hall**, installed in 2004 in what was previously a church, and **LSO St Luke's**, also in a church, which serves as a rehearsal space and second concert venue for the LSO.

Then there are the stalwarts: the **Royal Albert Hall**, home of the Proms, one of the highlights of the London cultural calendar; the pretty **Wigmore Hall**, its perfect acoustics ideally suited to chamber music; and the atmospheric **St Martin-in-the-Fields**, many of whose concerts are performed by candlelight.

As well as traditional venues like these, London's music schools, including **Guildhall School of Music & Drama**, the **Royal Academy of Music**, the **Royal College of Music** and **Trinity Laban**, hold regular concerts by their own pupils and established professional musicians. Dozens of lovely old churches, especially in the City, also host vibrant performances by young performers, often for free lunch-hour recitals.

Opera legends

Two venues reign supreme on the London opera scene: the **Royal Opera House** and the **Coliseum**, the headquarters of the English National Opera, which mixes established works with specially commissioned pieces such as the controversial operatic portrait of Muammar al-Gaddafi. All its productions are sung in English. The ROH, expensively done up at the turn of the millennium, sticks largely to traditional works.

Rock, pop & jazz

The capital's big venues for rock and pop are largely uninspiring; for the best concert-going, you're better off at smaller places like the riverside pub the **Bull's Head**, which offers a nice line in jazz. Much-loved old-timer Humphrey Lyttleton is a regular here. Of the medium-sized venues, the best is the **Shepherd's Bush Empire**, an old BBC theatre with good acoustics and

Shakespeare's Globe
21 New Globe Walk, SE1

catholic programming. Kentish Town's **Forum**, though tatty, isn't bad either, if only because it also has a good sound system, while the **Hammersmith Apollo** is still in good condition after a tidy-up some years ago. For notoriety alone, the number one is jazz temple, **Ronnie Scott's** – founded in 1959, now looks a little sprucer since the decorators set to in 2006. Jazzers who play here include Wynton Marsalis, Chick Corea, Kenny Garrett and Clint Eastwood's son, Kyle.

03

Theatre: the big hitters

It's fitting and reassuring that the London theatre scene should be so robust as this is, after all, the city in which Shakespeare plied his trade as well as being the professional home of Sir Laurence Olivier, Sir John Gielgud, the Redgraves and many other great thespians. The plethora of productions treading London's boards in any given month runs from glittery populist musicals to austere political drama, and the actors might be locals on the rise or Hollywood heroes shipped in to boost the glamour factor.

London's tightest-packed congregation of theatres is to be found in the West End. Those on Shaftesbury Avenue and many around Covent Garden are best known for musicals: venues like the **Queen's Theatre**, current home of long runner *Les Misérables*, the **Shaftesbury Theatre**,

Cambridge Theatre, Adelphi Theatre and the Theatre Royal Drury Lane, launch pad of the blockbuster stage version of *The Lord of the Rings*.

More highbrow are the celebrated **Royal Shakespeare Company**, which has its London residence at the refurbished Novello Theatre (the other is in Stratford-upon-Avon), and the **Old Vic**, whose high-profile artistic director since 2003 has been the American actor-director Kevin Spacey. Spacey's involvement has increased box-office takings, since he appears in two productions each season and directs a number of others.

Outside the West End, other theatrical powerhouses include the South Bank's **National Theatre** and Chelsea's **Royal Court**. The National, under creative director Nicholas Hytner, is on fine form, scoring big successes with plays like Alan Bennett's *The History Boys* and showcasing new drama by the likes of David Hare and Nicholas Wright. In the summer months an outdoor stage accommodates free performances of dance and street theatre. The Royal Court has been famous for hard-hitting, headline-grabbing drama ever since it opened in 1956 with John Osborne's *Look Back in Anger*. Contemporary playwrights whose work has been performed here include Tom Stoppard, Edward Bond, Christopher Hampton, Caryl Churchill and

Sarah Kane. The Barbican is another major supplier of first-class drama, often by touring international companies. Paris-based director Peter Brook, for example, is a regular here.

Theatre: small gems

The rest of London's theatrical landscape is made up of tinier venues with smallish budgets, which often belie their disproportionate creativity and hitting power. The **Young Vic**, founded in 1970, has added two smaller performance spaces to its main stage and continues to champion irreverent and iconoclastic writing and directing.

New playwrights, directors and actors are also much in evidence at the **Almeida** and **Donmar Warehouse**, both renowned for the polish of their productions and able to attract some big international stars such as Gwyneth Paltrow and Nicole Kidman.

Srill more contemporary writing is performed at **The Bush Theatre** and the **Soho Theatre**. Among the fringe venues, the **Menier Chocolate Factory** is an attractive spot in Southwark that puts on reliable mainstream productions. A regular supply of non-English-language productions is maintained by the **Goethe Institut** and the **Embassy of Japan**.

Shakespeare's Globe

The Globe theatre of Shakespeare's day, the 'wooden O' mentioned in *Henry V*, burned down in 1613. It was rebuilt in 1614, then shut by the Puritans in 1642 and destroyed two years later, but its fame, on the back of the Bard's, lived on. Since 1997, a replica known as **Shakespeare's Globe** (21 New Globe Walk, SE1; shakespeares-globe.org) has stood near the site of the original. The third Globe was the brainchild of late actor Sam Wanamaker and was built using as many period materials and building methods as possible, though sprinklers have been installed to prevent a repeat of 1613. Performances, lots of Shakespeare but also by a handful of contemporary writers, are historically authentic and often extremely good. The performance season at the Globe runs from May to October. Outside this period, visitors can take tours of the building (which includes the remains of the Rose Theatre), and there's an excellent year-round exhibition on the history of the area's theatres and the replica's construction.

The dance scene

The dance scene in London is amazingly vibrant and varied. Innovative contemporary dance companies exist in profusion, traditional ballet has a firm and highly respected place and the grass-roots appetite for classical and exotic disciplines can be seen in the huge range of classes on offer right across town.

03

Professional dance has its strongest footholds at the Barbican, **Sadler's Wells** and the Royal Opera House, and also at **The Place**, the **Laban Centre** and the **South Bank Centre**. Dance is now a big component of the Barbican's International Theatre Events festival (BICE). Sadler's Wells hosts the Jerwood Proms (part of Dance Umbrella) on top of its exciting year-round programme of shows by the likes of Sylvie Guillem, Pina Bausch, William Forsythe and the Rambert Dance Company, the country's flagship contemporary dance outfit. The ROH is home to the Royal Ballet, which helps keep traditional ballet alive and kicking, while opening up its repertory to experimental works by George Balanchine, Wayne McGregor and Christopher Wheeldon.

Elsewhere, look out for productions by McGregor's Random Dance, new talent Akram Khan, hip hop maestro Jonzi D, the English National Ballet and DV8 Physical Theatre.

Classical music

Barbican Centre
Silk St, EC2
⊖ Barbican
© 020 7638 4141
barbican.org.uk
✛ 8/W6

Cadogan Hall
5 Sloane Terrace, SW1
⊖ Sloane Square
© 020 7730 4500
cadoganhall.com
✛ 14/K14

Grosvenor Chapel
South Audley St, W1
⊖ Marble Arch
© 020 7499 1684
grosvenorchapel.org.uk
✛ 10/L10

Guildhall School of Music & Drama
Silk St, Barbican, EC2
⊖ Barbican
© 020 7628 2571
gsmd.ac.uk
✛ 8/W6

LSO St Luke's
161 Old St, EC1
⊖ Old Street
© 020 7490 3939
lso.co.uk/lsostlukes
✛ 4/X5

Royal Academy of Music
Marylebone Rd, NW1
⊖ Baker Street
© 020 7873 7373
ram.ac.uk
✛ 2/L5

Royal Albert Hall
Kensington Gore, SW7
⊖ South Kensington
© 020 7589 3203
royalalberthall.com
✛ 9-10/G12

Royal College of Music
Prince Consort Rd, SW7
⊖ Gloucester Road
© 020 7589 3643
rcm.ac.uk
✛ 9-10/G13

Royal Festival Hall
Southbank Centre, SE1
⊖ Waterloo
© 020 7921 0973
rfh.org.uk
✛ 11/S10

St James's Piccadilly
197 Piccadilly, W1
⊖ Piccadilly Circus
© 020 7381 0441
sjpconcerts.org
✛ 11/N10

St John's, Smith Square
Smith Sq, SW1
⊖ Westminster
© 020 7222 1061
sjss.org.uk
✛ 15/P14

St Martin-in-the-Fields
Trafalgar Sq, WC2
⊖ Charing Cross
© 020 7839 8362
stmartin-in-the-fields.org
✛ 11/P10

St Martin within Ludgate
40 Ludgate Hill, EC4
⊖ St Paul's
© 020 7248 6054
✛ 8/U8

Trinity Laban
Old Royal Naval College, SE10
⊖ Cutty Sark
© 020 8305 4444
tcm.ac.uk
⊕ Off map

Wigmore Hall
36 Wigmore St, W1
⊖ Bond Street
© 020 7935 2141
wigmore-hall.org.uk
✛ 6/K8

Opera legends

The Coliseum
St Martin's Lane, WC2
🚇 Charing Cross
📞 020 7632 8300
eno.org
🌐 7/P9

Royal Academy of Music
Marylebone Rd, NW1
🚇 Regent's Park
📞 020 7873 7373
ram.ac.uk
🌐 2/L5

Royal Opera House
Bow St, WC2
🚇 Covent Garden
📞 020 7304 4000
royalopera.org
🌐 7/Q8

Rock, pop & jazz

03

100 Club
100 Oxford St, W1
🚇 Oxford Circus
📞 020 7636 0933
the100club.co.uk
🌐 6/M8

Bull's Head
373 Lonsdale Rd, SW13
🚉 Barnes Bridge
📞 020 8876 5241
thebullshead.com
🌐 5/B8

Ronnie Scott's
47 Frith St, W1
🚇 Leicester Square
📞 020 7439 0747
ronniescotts.co.uk
🌐 7/O8

606 Club
90 Lots Rd, SW10
🚇 Fulham Broadway
📞 08713324104
606club.co.uk
🌐 Off map

Forum
9-17 Highgate Rd, NW5
🚇 Kentish Town
📞 020 7284 1001
meanfiddler.com
🌐 Off map

Shepherd's Bush Empire
Shepherd's Bush Green,
W12
🚇 Shepherd's Bush
📞 020 8354 3300
shepherds-bush-empire.
co.uk
🌐 Off map

Barfly Camden
49 Chalk Farm Rd,
NW1
🚇 Chalk Farm
📞 020 7691 4244
barflyclub.com
🌐 Off map

Hammersmith Apollo
Queen Caroline St, W6
🚇 Hammersmith
📞 020 8748 8660
getlive.co.uk
🌐 Off map

Union Chapel
Compton Terrace, N1
🚇 Highbury & Islington
📞 020 7226 1686
unionchapel.org.uk
🌐 Off map

Theatre: small gems

Almeida
Almeida St, N1
⊖ Angel
℃ 020 7359 4404
almeida.co.uk
⊕ 4/T1

The Bush Theatre
Shepherd's Bush Green, W12
⊖ Shepherd's Bush
℃ 020 7610 4224
bushtheatre.co.uk
⊕ Off map

Donmar Warehouse
41 Earlham St, WC2
⊖ Covent Gdn
℃ 020 8544 7412
donmarwarehouse.com
⊕ 7/P8

Embassy of Japan
101-104 Piccadilly, W1
⊖ Green Park
℃ 020 7465 6500
uk.emb-japan.go.jp
⊕ 11/M11

Gate Theatre
The Prince Albert, 11 Pembridge Rd, W11
⊖ Notting Hill Gate
℃ 020 7229 0706
gatetheatre.co.uk
⊕ 5/C9

Goethe Institut
50 Princes Gate, SW7
⊖ South Kensington
℃ 020 7596 4000
goethe.de
⊕ 10/H12

Menier Chocolate Factory
51-53 Southwark St, SE1
⊖ Borough
℃ 020 7907 7060
menierchocolatefactory.com
⊕ 12/V11

Soho Theatre
21 Dean St, W1
⊖ Tottenham Court Rd
℃ 020 7478 0100
sohotheatre.com
⊕ 7/V11

Young Vic
66 The Cut, SE1
⊖ Waterloo
℃ 020 7928 6363
youngvic.org
⊕ 12/T12

The dance scene

Laban Centre
Creekside, SE8
⊖ Deptford
℃ 020 8691 8600
laban.org
⊕ Off map

The Place
17 Duke's Rd, WC1
⊖ Euston
℃ 020 7121 1000
theplace.org.uk
⊕ 3/P4

Peacock Theatre
Portugal St, WC2
⊖ Holborn
℃ 020 7863 8198
sadlerswells.com
⊕ 7/R8

Sadler's Wells
Rosebery Av, EC1
⊖ Angel
℃ 020 7863 8000
sadlerswells.com
⊕ 4/T4

Southbank Centre
Belvedere Rd, SE1
⊖ Waterloo
℃ 020 7921 0973
⊕ 11/R11

Theatre: the big hitters

Adelphi Theatre
Strand, WC2
⊖ Charing Cross
℃ 020 7344 0055
adelphitheatre.co.uk
⊕ 11/Q10

National Theatre
South Bank, SE1
⊖ Waterloo
℃ 020 7452 3400
nationaltheatre.org.uk
⊕ 11/S10

Royal Court Theatre
Sloane Sq, SW1
⊖ Sloane Square
℃ 020 7565 5000
royalcourttheatre.com
⊕ 14/K14

Aldwych Theatre
Aldwych, WC2
⊖ Temple
℃ 020 7379 3367
aldwychtheatre.com
⊕ 7/R9

Novello Theatre
Aldwych, WC2
⊖ Charing Cross
℃ 0844 800 1110
rsc.org.uk
⊕ 7/R9

Shaftesbury Theatre
210 Shaftesbury Av, W1
⊖ Leicester Square
℃ 020 7379 5399
⊕ 7/O9

03

Cambridge Theatre
Earlham St, WC2
⊖ Covent Garden
℃ 020 7494 5080
cambridgetheatre.co.uk
⊕ 7/P8

Old Vic
Waterloo Rd, SE1
⊖ Waterloo
℃ 020 7928 7616
oldvictheatre.com
⊕ 11/T12

Royal Drury Lane
Catherine St, WC2
⊖ Covent Garden
℃ 020 7087 7559
theatreroyaldrurylanc.co.uk
⊕ 7/R9

Garrick Theatre
Charing Cross Rd, WC2
⊖ Leicester Squarc
℃ 0870 890 1104
garrick-theatre.com
⊕ 7/P8

Queen's Theatre
Shaftesbury Av, W1
⊖ Leicester Square
℃ 020 7494 5040
lesmis.com
⊕ 7/O9

Theatre Royal Haymarket
Haymarket, SW1
⊖ Piccadilly Circus
℃ 0870 901 3356
trh.co.uk
⊕ 11/O10

 See page 9 to scan the directory

INNOVATIVE ART
AND PHOTOGRAPHY

The Design Museum
Shad Thames, SE1

Previous page: White Cube
25-26 Mason's Yard, SW1

S ince Hoxton appeared on London's artistic map in the 1990s, London's position in the global arts market has been bullish, not to say dominant. The avalanche of global hits and hot new artists produced at this time were collectively dubbed the YBAs, Young British Artists, and many of this pack remain global superstars, among them Damien Hirst, Tracey Emin, Sam Taylor-Wood, Rachel Whiteread, Chris Ofili and the Chapman brothers. While the arts scene forks a little less lightning now than it did at the turn of the millennium, it is still in excellent health with major galleries expanding, refurbishing or moving, and significant new arrivals on the way.

04

Big and cutting edge

Some galleries have hogged the limelight for the past decade, and Jay Joplin's **White Cube** is one such example. It returned to the West End after a five-year absence with the opening in 2006 of a new outlet at Mason's Yard. Still out East is art lover's favourite, the **Whitechapel Art Gallery**, founded by one of the Victorian era's many philanthropists to bring art to the masses. It showed Picasso's *Guernica* in 1939, launched David Hockney and Gilbert & George, and continues to put on highly innovative, of-the-moment exhibitions. It is scheduled to reopen in 2008 after a major expansion and renovation.

Back in the centre of things, try the **Institute of Contemporary Arts**, known to Londoners simply as the ICA. Its stately accommodation is deceptive: the Institute defiantly challenges old-fashioned concepts of art, and it does this very well with shows that are always major events. Headline grabbing is de rigueur at another central operator, the **Saatchi Gallery**. Celebrated art collector Charles Saatchi was the man who got the Britart movement started in the first place. His gallery moved, in late 2007, from its landmark home in County Hall to the spacious, high-ceilinged rooms of the Duke of York's HQ on Sloane Square. The gallery occupies the whole of the huge building and has a well-stocked bookstore, educational facilities and a cool café/bar.

Dual-base galleries are increasingly popular. The US-owned **Gagosian**, the King's Cross colossus, opened a Mayfair adjunct to its home in WC1 in 2006 to please the edgy crowd and the more stylish Mayfair-ites. **Hauser & Wirth**, already the tenant of a large Mayfair former bank, opened two offshoots – a second Mayfair space and a huge former warehouse off Brick Lane.

Of more practical bent, the **Design Museum** is more parts exhibition space than museum in that it has no permanent collection as such, but the white building's shows of modern and contemporary design are engaging and well thought out. There's a small outdoor gallery called the Tank, which is used for installations.

Small and offbeat

So much for the big and the cutting-edge. The genteel flipside to the attention-grabbing shows at White Cube and co. is a venue like the **Bankside Gallery**, home to the Royal Society of Painter-Printmakers and the Royal Watercolour Society. Its annual exhibition calendar lines up expos by watercolour artists in March and October, and events by the painter-printmakers in May, as well as works by wood engravers every other August.

The former Cork Street art gallery hub is now dispersed around Mayfair and Soho, still the place to find international big names in galleries like **Stephen Friedman** or **Sadie Coles HQ**, whose eclectic yet on-the-pulse array includes John Bock, Richard Prince and Ugo Rondinone. Hackney and Bethnal Green are particularly good strolling grounds for smaller galleries exhibiting contemporary art like 2007 newcomer the **Wilkinson Gallery**, the prestigious **Maureen Paley** gallery, outlet for Turner Prize winners Wolfgang

04

Institute of Contemporary Arts
The Mall, SW1

Tillmans and Gillian Wearing; and smart young galleries like **Modern Art** and **Vilma Gold**.

The appearance of big not-for-profit galleries is an intriguing mini trend. The **Louise T Blouin Institute** was opened by the owner of the LTB group of companies, publisher of *Art+Auction* and *Modern Painters* magazines. Her new venture is housed in a pre-war coachworks in Shepherd's Bush, and alongside the exhibition space runs a cinema, a café and a conference centre. Artists shown here have included James Turrell and Marc Quinn. In a similar vein is **Parasol Unit** in Islington, a former warehouse transformed into a two-floor exhibition space that shows artworks by both rising star and big-name artists.

Architecture and photography

Architectural exhibitions are largely the preserve of the **Architectural Association** and the prestigious **Royal Institute of British Architects**. The Architectural Association holds shows, talks and events, and is the venue for the AA School's summer graduation show. The RIBA, which also has a gallery at the V&A, puts on exhibitions and lectures at its Marylebone HQ.

There are few galleries dedicated to photography in London. Two outstanding spaces are **Michael Hoppen**

04

Seasonal art fairs

Do bear in mind that the contemporary arts scene is richer at some periods of the year than others. Spring and autumn are the best seasons to make the art gallery rounds, whereas there's very little worth seeing over the Christmas and New Year break, in late July and in August.

That said, the summer drought is slaked to some extent by the art schools' graduation shows. Of particular note are those at the **Royal College of Art** and **Chelsea College of Art & Design**. The highlight of the autumn season is the **Frieze Art Fair** in October, which had its first edition in 2003 and has since been the pivot around which the entire contemporary arts calendar revolves. Exhibitors have included London galleries such as Maureen Paley and White Cube, Berlin's Galerie Neu and Contemporary Fine Arts, and New Yorkers Mary Boone and Matthew Marks.

The fashionable Frieze Art Fair has also sparked off a parallel showcase for the city's more youthful galleries: the **Zoo Art Fair** in the park at London Zoo. *(See Chapter Nine.)*

Gallery in Chelsea and the **Photographer's Gallery** in Covent Garden; the latter is moving in 2008 to prestigious new premises in Ramillies Street, just around the corner from its current address. It hosts a steady stream of varied exhibitions on all sorts of subjects by photographers from all over the world. Photos on show can be historic, contemporary, documentary, experimental, professional or amateur but they're always well curated. The Michael Hoppen Gallery occupies three floors and displays a mix of photography spanning the 19th century to the present day. Look out for exhibitions of work by Cecil Beaton, Erwin Blumenfeld, Jacques-Henri Lartigue, Bill Brandt, Sarah Moon, Irving Penn, William Klein and many more greats.

04

Getty Images off Oxford Street is another must for photography aficionados. Delve into its vast Hulton Getty Archive to choose the image of your dreams and its dark room team will print the photo to your specifications, by hand. The archive comprises over 300 separate collections and around 40 million negatives. Exhibitions, such as a celebration of the *Picture Post,* are held regularly.

Big and cutting edge

Design Museum
Shad Thames, SE1
⊖ Tower Hill
① 020 7403 6933
designmuseum.org
⊕ 12/Z11

Gagosian
6-24 Britannia St, WC1
⊖ King's Cross
① 020 7841 9960
gagosian.com
⊕ 3/R3

Haunch of Venison
6 Haunch of Venison
Yard, W1
⊖ Bond Street
① 020 7495 5050
haunchofvenison.com
⊕ 6/M8

Hauser & Wirth London
196a Piccadilly, W1
⊖ Piccadilly Circus
① 020 7287 2300
hauserwirth.com
⊕ 11/N10

Hayward Gallery
South Bank Centre,
Belvedere Rd, SE1
⊖ Waterloo
① 020 7921 0813
southbankcentre.co.uk
⊕ 11/S10

**Institute of Contemporary
Arts (ICA)**
The Mall, SW1
⊖ Charing Cross
① 020 7930 3647
ica.org.uk
⊕ 11/O11

Lisson Gallery
29 & 52-54 Bell St, NW1
⊖ Edgware Road
① 020 7724 2739
lissongallery.com
⊕ 6/H6

Saatchi Gallery
Duke of York's
Headquarters, SW1
⊖ Sloane Square
① 020 7928 8195
saatchi-gallery.co.uk
⊕ 14/J15

Waddington Galleries
11 Cork St, W1
⊖ Green Park
① 020 7437 8611
waddington-galleries.com
⊕ 6-7/N9

Wapping Project
Wapping Power Station,
Wapping Wall, E1
⊖ Wapping
① 020 7680 2080
thewappingproject.com
⊕ Off map

Whitechapel Art Gallery
80 Whitechapel High St, E1
⊖ Aldgate East
① 020 7522 7878
whitechapel.org
⊕ 8/Z8

White Cube
25-26 Mason's Yard, SW1
⊖ Piccadilly Circus
① 020 7930 5373
whitecube.com
⊕ 11/N10

Small and offbeat

Anthony Reynolds
60 Gt Marlborough St, W1
⊖ Oxford Circus
① 020 7439 2201
anthonyreynolds.com
⊕ 7/N8

The Approach
47 Approach Rd, E2
⊖ Bethnal Green
① 020 8983 3878
theapproach.co.uk
⊕ Off map

Bankside Gallery
48 Hopton St, SE1
⊖ Southwark
① 020 7928 7521
banksidegallery.com
⊕ 12/U10

Crafts Council Gallery
44a Pentonville Rd, N1
⊖ Angel
ⓒ 020 7278 7700
craftscouncil.org.uk
⊕ 3/R3

Flowers East
82 Kingsland Rd, E2
⊖ Old Street
ⓒ 020 7920 7777
flowerseast.com
⊕ 4/Z3

Frith Street Gallery
17-18 Golden Sq, W1
⊖ Piccadilly Circus
ⓒ 020 7494 1550
frithstreetgallery.com
⊕ 6-7/N9

Hales Gallery
7 Bethnal Green Rd, E1
⊖ Liverpool Street
ⓒ 020 7033 1938
halesgallery.com
⊕ 4/7.5

Jerwood Space
171 Union St, SE1
⊖ Southwark
ⓒ 020 7654 0171
jerwoodspace.co.uk
⊕ 12/U11

Louise T Blouin Institute
3 Olaf St, W11
⊖ Latimer Road
ⓒ 020 7985 9600
ltbfoundation.org
⊕ Off map

Maureen Paley
21 Herald St, E2
⊖ Bethnal Green
ⓒ 020 7729 4112
maureenpaley.com
⊕ Off map

Modern Art
7A & 10 Vyner St, E2
⊖ Bethnal Green
ⓒ 020 8980 7742
stuartshavemodernart.com
⊕ Off map

Monika Sprüth & Philomene Magers
7A Grafton St, W1
Bond Street
020 7408 1613
⊕ 6/M9

Parasol Unit
14 Wharf Rd, N1
⊖ Angel
ⓒ 020 7490 7373
parasol-unit.org
⊕ 4/V3

Riflemaker
79 Beak St, W1
⊖ Piccadilly Circus
ⓒ 020 7439 0000
riflemaker.org
⊕ 6-7/N9

Sadie Coles HQ
35 Heddon St, W1
⊖ Piccadilly Circus
ⓒ 020 7434 2227
sadiecoles.com
⊕ 6-7/N9

Simon Lee
12 Berkeley St, W1
⊖ Green Park
ⓒ 020 7491 0100
simonleegallery.com
⊕ 11/M10

Stephen Friedman
25 Old Burlington St, W1
⊖ Green Park
ⓒ 020 7494 1434
stephenfriedman.com
⊕ 6-7/N9

Timothy Taylor Gallery
24 Dering St, W1
⊖ Bond Street
ⓒ 020 7409 3344
timothytaylorgallery.com
⊕ 6/M8

04

Wapping Project
Wapping Wall, E1

Small and offbeat (continued)

Victoria Miro
16 Wharf Rd, N1
⊖ Angel
© 020 7336 8109
victoria-miro.com
⊕ 4/V3

Vilma Gold
25B Vyner St, E2
⊖ Bethnal Green
© 020 8981 3344
vilmagold.com
⊕ Off map

Wilkinson Gallery
242 Cambridge Heath
Rd, E2
⊖ Bethnal Green
© 020 8980 2662
wilkinsongallery.com
⊕ Off map

Seasonal art fairs

Frieze Art Fair
Mid October
Regent's Park, NW1
⊖ Regent's Park
© 020 7833 7270
friezeartfair.com
⊕ 2/K3

**Royal College of Art
Summer Show**
May–July
Kensington Gore, SW7
⊖ Gloucester Road
© 020 7590 4444
rca.ac.uk
⊕ 9-10/G12

Zoo Art Fair
Mid October
London Zoo, NW1
⊖ Camden Town
© 020 8964 3272
zooartfair.com
⊕ 2/K2

04

Architecture and photography

**Architectural
Association**
36 Bedford Sq, WC1
⊖ Tottenham Court Rd
© 020 7887 4000
aaschool.ac.uk
⊕ 7/P7

**Michael Hoppen
Gallery**
3 Jubilee Pl, SW3
⊖ Sloane Square
© 020 7352 4499
michaelhoppengallery.com
⊕ 14/I16

Proud Camden Moss
Stables Market, Chalk
Farm Rd, NW1
⊖ Chalk Farm
© 020 7482 3867
proud.co.uk
⊕ Off map

Getty Images
36 East Castle St, W1
⊖ Oxford Circus
© 020 7291 5380
gettyimages.com/archival
⊕ 7/N8

Photographer's Gallery
5 & 8 Great Newport
St, WC2
⊖ Leicester Square
© 020 7831 1772
photonet.org.uk
⊕ 7/P9

**Royal Institute of
British Architects**
66 Portland Pl, W1
⊖ Great Portland St
© 020 7580 5533
architecture.com
⊕ 6/M6

See page 9
to scan the
directory

MUSEUMS AND
CULTURAL COLLECTIONS

British Museum
Great Russell St, WC1

Previous page: Design Museum
28 Shad Thames, SE1

Not many capitals can match the fame, variety and sheer quantity of London's artistic treasures. Few cities have enjoyed London's historic importance in world trade, or the enlightened generosity of its benefactors and philanthropists, nor can many cities feed as much as London does on the British fondness for collecting things, from Renaissance oil paintings to 1950's soap packets. In addition, London feels like a giant museum *in toto*, a centuries-old accumulation of architecture, public sculpture, botany, fixtures and fittings, right down to the iconic Routemaster buses and red letter boxes. Walk around it and marvel.

05

Unmissable national collections

Of the big-hitter museums, none is bigger than the **British Museum**: it's the city's most visited attraction and its enormous collection covers world cultures from prehistory to the present. It has the Rosetta Stone, the Elgin Marbles, a wealth of Assyrian, Mesopotamian and ancient Egyptian statuary, some awe-inspiring Japanese swords, Rembrandt etchings and objects from Rome, Greece and the Pacific Islands. Robert Smirke's neo-classical edifice, built in 1847, is impressive on its own and, at the turn of the 21st century, the Great Court was beautifully restored and roofed over with an undulating array of glass lozenges by Norman Foster.

Almost as capacious is the **National Gallery**, which contains over 2,000 priceless paintings. Standout works include Constable's *The Hay Wain*, Van Gogh's *Chair* and iconic art by Monet, Seurat, Hogarth, Gainsborough and Reynolds. The Sainsbury Wing opened in 1991 to focus on the early Renaissance period, especially in Holland and Italy. Crivelli's breathtakingly ornate study in perspective, *The Annunciation with Saint Emidius,* is not to be missed. Just don't attempt to see too much in one go.

Around the corner from the National is the **National Portrait Gallery**, whose collections of royals, rogues, heroes and forgotten notables are arranged in chronological order with the oldest at the top. The predominant medium is oil painting, but photography also gets a showing, especially in the temporary exhibitions.

London's second largest collection of historic Western art after the National is **Tate Britain**, the difference being that the art here is exclusively British, five centuries of it. There's an unrivalled host of works by Turner and paintings by the Pre-Raphaelites, as well as art by Bacon, Moore and Reynolds, and three rooms dedicated to Constable. The oldest works date from the 16th century, but contemporary painters like Lucian Freud and David Hockney are represented as well.

More British art can be seen in the permanent collections of the **Royal Academy of Arts**: paintings by Constable, Reynolds, Turner, Millais and Hockney, as well as sculptures, drawings, prints, photos and plaster casts.

Presenting a combination of canvasses and curios is the incomparable **Victoria & Albert Museum** (V&A). Paintings, textiles, ceramics, jewellery and *objets d'art* from across the globe are grouped by era, theme or country of origin, and include the finest selection of Italian Renaissance statues outside Italy.

05

The fashion galleries display elaborate costumes from the 18th century to the present day, the photography gallery has half a million photos; a selection of which are on show at any one time whereas the architecture gallery features models, plans and screens showing short documentaries. The Victoria & Albert Museum also hosts shows organized by the Crafts Council (craftscouncil.org.uk), such as the annual Collect crafts fair *(see Chapter Nine)*.

Tate Modern
Bankside, SE1

Significant collections

The **Courtauld Institute of Art Gallery**, inside Somerset House, is particularly strong on the Impressionists like Van Gogh's *Self-portrait with Bandaged Ear*, and paintings by Gauguin, Renoir, Degas, Manet and Monet, as well as works by Rubens and 20th century artists such as Matisse and Modigliani. Also in the same building are the **Hermitage Rooms**, which host a changing line-up of exhibits on anything from paintings to jewels from St Petersburg's Winter Palace, all in settings designed to mimic the Russian original.

At the **Guildhall Art Gallery**, the most unmissable piece is the colossal *Siege of Gibraltar* by the American painter John Copley, which took five years to finish and measures 24 feet by nearly 18 feet. Elsewhere in the basement are Pre-Raphaelite paintings, works by Reynolds and Constable, sculptures, and the ruins of a Roman amphitheatre.

Small can also be beautiful and the **Dulwich Picture Gallery** is a prime example of this concept. Dubbed "the most beautiful small art gallery in the world" by the *Sunday Telegraph*, it occupies a building by Sir John Soane, the 18th and 19th century architect responsible for the Bank of England, and houses works by Rembrandt, Raphael, Rubens, Van Dyck and Poussin.

05

Apsley House on Hyde Park Corner contains china, tableware and a variety of intriguing knick-knacks. In its crimson and gilt picture gallery hangs Goya's portrait of the Duke of Wellington, a Velásquez and a Correggio. Ask a member of the staff to show you the workings of the mirrors.

Personal collections

One of the capital's most charming museums is the **Wallace Collection**. The building is an 18th century mansion of conspicuous nobility, and the collection it houses was assembled by the 19th century philanthropist Sir Richard Wallace. Franz Hals's *Laughing Cavalier*, other fabulous paintings by Gainsborough, Reynolds, Boucher, Velázquez, and a vast amount of Louis XIV and Louis XV furniture, antique armour, porcelain and assorted *objets d'art* all vie for attention here.

Architect Sir John Soane was an obsessive collector and stuffed his house with a stunning jumble of sculpture, furniture and paintings. He threw it open during his lifetime to discerning members of the public and the result is the **Sir John Soane's Museum**. Among the paintings on show are works by Canaletto, Hogarth and Turner; there are busts and Egyptian antiquities, including an astonishing alabaster sarcophagus made for a 19th dynasty pharaoh.

Private collections are difficult, but not impossible, to see. One of the most intriguing is **Clarence House**, home of the Prince of Wales and his sons, on The Mall. During the summer, parts of the palatial house are open to the public. The Queen Mother's art collection is world renowned, and works by Augustus John and John Piper as well as an array of Fabergé eggs are also displayed. Tickets must be booked in advance, and they always sell out fast. Parts of other collections are visitable during Open House *(see Chapter Nine)*.

20th century and contemporary

05

The **Dalí Universe**, curated by Benjamin Levi, a friend of the artist himself, showcases watercolours, sculptures, the famous red lips sofa and the painting from *Spellbound*, as well as etchings and lithographs. The collection, totalling around 500 works, gives a vivid insight into the artist's mind. A gallery adjunct exhibits works by contemporary artists.

The **Estorick Collection of Modern Italian Art** showcases the art acquired by American writer-theorist Eric Estorick. Situated in a Georgian townhouse in picturesque Canonbury, it's the only gallery dedicated to 20th century Italian art in the British Isles. Here you'll find works by the Futurists and pieces by Carra, Russolo and Severini, as well as sculptures by Rosso and Marini.

William Morris Gallery
Lloyd Park, Forest Rd, E17

Decoration and design

The **William Morris Gallery** occupies the former home of the artist-designer. His work on paper, fabric, ceramics and stained glass are all on show here in striking style, as well as designs produced by his disciples. Like the V&A, **Kensington Palace** has a collection of historic dresses and costumes; more textiles can be seen in the **Horniman Museum**, which also has a rich and eccentric collection of anthropological and natural history exhibits, as well as exotic costumes and masks from its collection of 6,500 items.

Collections of curiosities

05

The British are notoriously fond of museums devoted to the offbeat and the peculiar. The **Clockmakers' Museum** is a great horological orchestra of clocks and watches made by still-active craft guild the Worshipful Company of Clockmakers of London. Many of the exhibits are kept wound up, ticking and tocking and chiming away in wonderful contentment. The collection includes sundials, marine chronometers and pieces by contemporary British watchmakers.

Another niche interest museum is the **Fan Museum**, home to the largest collection of fans in the world. It has more than 3,500 exhibits, though only a small proportion is shown at one time; the oldest dates from the 11th century.

Artistic powerhouse

The **Tate Modern**, younger sister of Tate Britain, is Britain's national museum of international modern art. It was an instant hit when it opened in 2000 – one of the global art world's biggest events and a central plank of Britain's claims to be a revived cultural nation. The building was formerly a power station, and its soaring chimney and massive dimensions impress before you even enter. Its permanent collection features Picasso, Matisse, Rothko, Pollock, Warhol and more. In 2006 the whole museum was rehung, so art is now grouped by movement (Cubism, Surrealism, Vorticism, Pop Art) rather than by subject matter. The colossal Turbine Hall, which once housed the electricity generators, is the venue for large-scale, specially commissioned temporary exhibits. A glass pyramid extension dedicated to photography and video, which will increase the display space by 60 per cent, is set to open in 2012. In summer the handy Tate to Tate river shuttle operates every 20 minutes between Tates Britain and Modern and the boat used is distinctively covered in a spotted Damien Hirst design.

Sharing its Somerset House premises with the Courtauld and the Hermitage Rooms is the **Gilbert Collection**. Donated to the nation in 1996, millionaire Sir Arthur Gilbert's collection of gold and silverware is a dragon's hoard of British silver. Roman enamel mosaics and gold boxes, candlesticks, religious icons and trinkets from Russia, India and Italy are also showcased.

True to the irreverent history of its Bloomsbury setting, the **Cartoon Museum** displays the best of British cartoon art, chronologically, from the 18th century to the present day. Hogarth, naturally, is represented along with more recent exponents such as David Low, Gerald Scarfe and active contemporary satirists like the *Guardian*'s Steve Bell. The first floor is given over to British comic art like Rupert Bear and Dan Dare.

05

Retrogressive nursery pleasures, more likely to appeal to grown-ups than children, are to be had at **Pollock's Toy Museum**, which occupies a suitably eccentric Georgian townhouse. Nostalgia is also the stock in trade of the **Museum of Brands, Packaging & Advertising**, a good showcase of the commercial illustrator's art with a century's worth of largely British ad posters and old soap packets that would have been daily sights when granny was a young girl.

Unmissable national collections

British Museum
Great Russell St, WC1
⊖ Tottenham Court Rd
ⓒ 020 7636 1555
thebritishmuseum.ac.uk
⊕ 7/Q7

National Gallery
Trafalgar Sq, WC2
⊖ Charing Cross
ⓒ 020 7747 2885
nationalgallery.org.uk
⊕ 11/P10

National Portrait Gallery
2 St Martin's Pl, WC2
⊖ Charing Cross
ⓒ 020 7306 0055
npg.org.uk
⊕ 11/P10

Royal Academy of Arts
Burlington House,
Piccadilly, W1
⊖ Piccadilly Circus
ⓒ 020 7300 8000
royalacademy.org.uk
⊕ 11/N10

Tate Britain
Millbank, SW1
⊖ Pimlico
ⓒ 020 7887 8000
tate.org.uk
⊕ 15/P16

Victoria & Albert Museum
Cromwell Rd, SW7
⊖ South Kensington
ⓒ 020 7942 2000
vam.ac.uk
⊕ 9-13/H14

Significant collections

Apsley House
Hyde Park Corner, W1
⊖ Hyde Park Corner
ⓒ 020 7499 5676
english-heritage.org.uk
⊕ 10/K12

Courtauld Institute of Art Gallery
Somerset House, Strand, WC2
⊖ Temple
ⓒ 020 7848 2526
courtauld.ac.uk/gallery
⊕ 11/Q10

Dulwich Picture Gallery
Gallery Rd, SE21
≋ North Dulwich
ⓒ 020 8693 5254
dulwichpicture
gallery.org.uk
⊕ Off map

Guildhall Art Gallery
Guildhall Yard, EC2
⊖ St Paul's
ⓒ 020 7332 3700
guildhall-art-gallery.org.uk
⊕ 8/W8

Hermitage Rooms
Somerset House,
Strand, WC2
⊖ Temple
ⓒ 020 7845 4630
hermitagerooms.co.uk
⊕ 11/Q10

Kenwood House
Hampstead Lane, NW3
⊖ Hampstead
ⓒ 020 8348 1286
english-heritage.org.uk
⊕ Off map

Personal collections

Clarence House
The Mall, SW1
⊖ Green Park
© 020 7766 7303
royalcollection.org.uk
⊕ 11/011

Sir John Soane's Museum
13 Lincoln's Inn Fields,
WC2
⊖ Holborn
© 020 7405 2107
soane.org
⊕ 7/R7

Wallace Collection
Hertford Hse,
Manchester Sq, W1
⊖ Bond Street
© 020 7935 0687
wallacecollection.org
⊕ 6/K7

20th century and contemporary

Dalí Universe
County Hall, SE1
⊖ Waterloo
© 020 7620 2720
daliuniverse.com
⊕ 7/R9

**Estorick Collection of
Modern Italian Art**
39a Canonbury Sq, N1
⊖ Highbury & Islington
© 020 7704 9522
estorickcollection.com
⊕ Off map

Tate Modern
Bankside, SE1
⊖ Blackfriars
© 020 7401 5120
tate.org.uk
⊕ 8/V10

05

Decoration and design

Design Museum
28 Shad Thames, SE1
⊖ London Bridge
© 0870 909 9009
designmuseum.org
⊕ 12/Z11

Horniman Museum
100 London Rd, SE23
⊖ Forest Hill
© 020 8699 1872
horniman.ac.uk
⊕ Off map

Leighton House Museum
12 Holland Park Rd, W14
⊖ High St Kensington
© 020 7602 3316
rbkc.gov.uk/
leightonhousemuseum
⊕ 9/B13

Geffrye Museum
136 Kingsland Rd, E2
⊖ Old Street
© 020 7739 9893
geffrye-museum.org.uk
⊕ 4/Z3

Kensington Palace
Kensington Gdns, W8
⊖ Queensway
© 020 7937 9561
hrp.org.uk
⊕ 9/B13

William Morris Gallery
Lloyd Park, Forest Rd, E17
⊖ Walthamstow Central
© 020 8527 3782
lbwf.gov.uk/wmg
⊕ Off map

Sir John Soane's Museum
13 Lincoln's Inn Fields, WC2

Collections of curiosities

Cartoon Museum
35 Little Russell St, WC1
⊖ Tottenham Court Rd
© 020 7580 8155
cartoonmuseum.org
⊕ 7/Q7

Freud Museum
20 Maresfield Gdns,
NW3
⊖ Finchley Rd
© 020 7435 2002
freud.org.uk
⊕ Off map

**Old Operating Theatre
Museum**
9a St Thomas St, SE1
⊖ London Bridge
© 020 7188 2679
thegarret.org.uk
⊕ 12/W11

Clockmaker's Museum
Guildhall Library,
Aldermanbury, EC2
⊖ Bank
© 020 7332 1868
clockmakers.org
⊕ 8/W8

Gilbert Collection
Somerset House, Strand,
WC2
⊖ Temple
© 020 7420 9400
gilbert-collection.org.uk
⊕ 11/Q10

Pollock's Toy Museum
1 Scala St, W1
⊖ Goodge Street
© 020 7636 3452
pollockstoymuseum.com
⊕ 7/O7

05

Fan Museum
12 Crooms Hill, SE10
≈ Cutty Sark
© 020 8305 1441
fan-museum.org
⊕ Off map

**Museum of Brands,
Packaging & Advertising**
Colville Mews, Lonsdale
Rd, W11
⊖ Notting Hill Gate
© 020 7908 0880
museumofbrands.com
⊕ 5/B8

**V & A Museum of
Childhood**
Cambridge Heath, E2
⊖ Bethnal Green
© 020 8983 5200
vam.ac.uk.moc
⊕ Off map

See page 9
to scan the
directory

MOVIE HOUSES
AND SCREENING ROOMS

Electric Cinema
191 Portobello Rd, W11

Previous page: Screen on the Green
83 Upper St, N1

L ondon's river of cinematic delight flows broad and deep. The multi-screen monsters, all vast screens and state-of-the-art sound, are present and correct. Still, the best film-going to be had is to be had at smaller cinemas, such as the **Electric Cinema** and the **Renoir**, which are not afraid to show less mainstream non-Hollywood works.

Independent picture houses

The **Curzon** mini-chain has footholds in Soho and Mayfair, both of which channel a steady stream of excellent arthouse and indie fare in English and other languages, beefed up by frequent Q&A sessions. The Soho branch has a lobby café serving delicious Konditor & Cook cakes and, in the basement, the best bar on Shaftesbury Avenue. You don't even have to buy a ticket to drink there. The **Chelsea Cinema**, the **Clapham Picture House** and the **Notting Hill Coronet** follow closely on the Curzon's heels.

The **Screen on the Green** has the best old-fashioned neon billboard in town and some of the comfiest seating anywhere in London, while the programmers tend to interleave mainstream and independent.

06

BFI Southbank

The three-screen National Film Theatre relaunched in 2007 with a new look, new features and a new name: **BFI Southbank** (South Bank, SE1; www.bfi.org.uk). It's now a world-class place in which to see a film. Whereas the old NFT had its entrance under Waterloo Bridge, a gloomy point of ingress even on a summer day, BFI Southbank has a new front door surrounded by a white-lit 'lightbox' and a glass-walled foyer. New facilities include the BFI Mediatheque, where visitors can peruse the BFI film and TV archives via cutting-edge video consoles, an exhibition space devoted to film-related shows by contemporary artists, and a café-bar area equipped with Wi-Fi. The much-missed bookstore has also made a welcome return. What hasn't changed, however, is unbeatable programming at what is still London's most prestigious picture house. Everything from retrospectives of the great masters to documentaries to recent offbeat fiction films can be found on show here. Q&A sessions are another regular attraction. Guests have included Pedro Almodóvar, Penelope Cruz and Catherine Deneuve.

The **Electric Cinema** is one of the city's oldest picture houses and has gradually been done up to the point where it's now one of the most trendy and luxurious, with leather armchairs and romantic two-seater sofas. In a similar upmarket bracket is the **Everyman Cinema**, which gives its audience the choice of two screening lounges equipped with footstools, plush designer style upholstery, wine coolers and a full food menu.

Arthouse and repertoire

There's a commendably generous supply of work from outside the English-speaking mainstream. Hollywood may take the lion's share of the box office, but the lion's share of enthusiasm belongs to the unorthodox and unusual movies shown in independent cinemas and cultural centres. The **Barbican Centre** has three screens, which it uses to show new world and indie releases with a smattering of classics. It also regularly reels in big stars to discuss their work, Michel Piccoli to talk about filming with Buñuel, for example, as does the **Ciné Lumière**, whose programming largely consists of French films.

The other foreign cultural institutions function in a similar way. The **Embassy of Japan** holds thrice-yearly seasons of old and new Japanese films that you're unlikely to see elsewhere, and all for free, though

06

Goethe Institut
50 Princes Gate, SW7

you need to book well in advance via the website. The **Goethe Institut** and the **Istituto Italiano di Cultura** screen German and Italian films respectively.

Mainstream cinemas

The multiplexes and chain cinemas often have the most impressive technical specs. Think big reverberating sounds, giant screens, vast auditoriums, incredible picture quality and digital projectors. The **Odeon** and **Cineworld** chains dominate the market in US blockbusters and broad-appeal comedies and each runs multiplexes across the city, though there's little to tell them apart. Such mainstream picture houses win through the convenience born of proliferation, and they're most densely concentrated around Leicester Square. The **Empire** stands out from the herd for its regular premieres of Bollywood blockbusters.

Private screening rooms

Movie-going with the sweet smell of exclusivity is a fad that's quickly catching on. A swelling band of luxury and boutique hotels are kitting themselves out with screening facilities. **One Aldwych**, whose 30-seat screening room boasts stylish Italian-made leather seats, doesn't even restrict screenings to hotel guests. Its Saturday and Sunday Movies on the Menu programme serves up a three-course lunch or dinner in the Axis restaurant after which the sated film-goers adjourn to the auditorium,

06

Home cinema sources

No movie buff these days gets fixes from big screens alone but, conversely, London's terrific array of goods for the home cinema devotee wouldn't be half what it is without the city's movie houses feeding demand. In the words of Martin Scorsese, the antidote to film is more film, which makes **Fopp** on Tottenham Court Road a veritable institute of toxicology. It's a sleek superstore stocked with thousands of DVDs, plus a selection of filmmaker biographies and readable genre studies, to say nothing of soundtracks and CDs in other musical categories. Fopp gives big discounts to almost everything, and the range of titles on its shelves is excellent, world cinema included.

For books, visit Covent Garden's **Offstage Theatre & Film Bookshop**, in a snug basement space, or nearby **Cinema Store**. The latter stocks the latest film tomes, posters, movie star figurines and autographed photographs, and brings in film makers and actors for regular signings.

where any lingering hunger is zapped with complimentary popcorn and champagne. The films tend to be classics – *Vertigo*, *Some Like It Hot*, and so on. Booking can be done by phone or the website.

Once you've cut your teeth with Movies on the Menu, the next step is to hire a screening room, which means you can choose the programming yourself. Three hotels in the Firmdale group – **Soho Hotel**, **Charlotte Street Hotel** and **Covent Garden Hotel** – have swish mini cinemas, and all can be hired for private functions.

If the gathering is to be large, you'll need the headquarters of the British Academy of Film and Television Arts (BAFTA) at **195 Piccadilly**. It has a 213-seat screening facility equipped with a digital projector so advanced that only a handful exist in the entire country.

06

Smaller but unbeatably romantic is the **Rex Cinema & Bar** in the British film industry's heartland, Soho. Its gorgeous 1930's-style private bar is the ideal foil to its more formal, deeply luxurious 75-seat cinema.

Independent picture houses

Chelsea Cinema
206 King's Rd, SW3
⊖ Sloane Sq
© 020 7351 3742
artificial-eye.com
⊕ 14/H17

Clapham Picturehouse
76 Venn St, SW4
⊖ Clapham Common
© 0870 755 0061
picturehouses.co.uk
⊕ Off map

Curzon Mayfair
38 Curzon St, W1
⊖ Green Park
© 020 7495 0501
curzoncinemas.com
⊕ 10/L11

Curzon Soho
99 Shaftesbury Av, W1
⊖ Leicester Square
© 020 7292 1686
curzoncinemas.com
⊕ 7/O9

Electric Cinema
191 Portobello Rd, W11
⊖ Ladbroke Grove
© 020 7908 9696
the-electric.co.uk
⊕ 5/A6

Everyman Cinema
5 Hollybush Vale, NW3
⊖ Hampstead
© 020 7435 1600
everymancinema.com
⊕ Off map

Notting Hill Coronet
103 Notting Hill Gate, W11
⊖ Notting Hill Gate
© 020 7727 6705
coronet.org
⊕ 9/C10

Phoenix
52 High Road, N2
⊖ East Finchley
© 020 8444 6789
phoenixcinema.co.uk
⊕ Off map

Prince Charles
7 Leicester Pl, WC2
⊖ Leicester Square
© 0870 811 2559
princecharlescinema.com
⊕ 7/P9

Renoir
Brunswick Centre, WC1
⊖ Russell Square
© 020 7837 8402
curzoncinemas.com
⊕ 3/Q5

Richmond Filmhouse
3 Water Lane, Richmond,
⊖ Richmond
© 0871 223 8121
richmondfilmhouse.co.uk
⊕ Off map

Ritzy Picture House
Coldharbour Lane, SW2
⊖ Brixton
© 0870 755 0062
ritzycinema.co.uk
⊕ Off map

Screen on Baker Street
96-98 Baker St, W1
⊖ Baker Street
© 020 7935 2772
screencinemas.co.uk
⊕ 6/K6

Screen on the Green
83 Upper St, N1
⊖ Angel
© 020 7226 3520
screencinemas.co.uk
⊕ 4/T2

Tricycle Cinema
269 Kilburn High Rd, NW6
⊖ Kilburn
© 020 7328 1900
tricycle.co.uk
⊕ 1/D1

Arthouse and repertoire

Barbican
Silk St, EC2
⊖ Barbican
☏ 020 7382 7000
barbican.org.uk
⊕ 8/W6

Ciné Lumière
Institut Français, 17
Queensbury Pl, SW7
⊖ South Kensington
☏ 020 7073 1350
⊕ 13/G14

Embassy of Japan
101-104 Piccadilly, W1
⊖ Green Park
☏ 020 7465 6500
uk.emb-japan.go.jp
⊕ 11/M11

Goethe Institut
50 Princes Gate, SW7
⊖ South Kensington
☏ 020 7596 4000
goethe.de
⊕ 10/H12

ICA Cinema
The Mall, SW1
⊖ Charing Cross
☏ 020 7930 6393
ica.org.uk
⊕ 11/O11

Istituto Italiano di Cultura
39 Belgrave Sq, SW1
⊖ Hyde Park Corner
☏ 020 7235 1461
icilondon.esteri.it
⊕ 10/K13

Mainstream cinemas

Cineworld
7-14 Coventry St, W1
⊖ Piccadilly Circus
☏ 020 7434 0032
cineworld.co.uk
⊕ 7/O9

Empire
4 6 Leicester Sq, WC2
⊖ Leicester Square
☏ 020 7734 7123
empirecinemas.co.uk
⊕ 7/P9

Odeon
40 Leicester Sq, WC2
⊖ Leicester Square
☏ 020 7930 6111
odeon.co.uk
⊕ 7/P9

06

Curzon Mayfair
38 Curzon St, W1

BAFTA
195 Piccadilly, W1

Home cinema sources

Cinema Store
4 Upper St Martin's
Lane, WC2
⊖ Leicester Square
ⓒ 020 7379 7895
the-cinema-store.com
⊕ 7/P9

Fopp
220-224 Tottenham
Court Rd, W1
⊖ Goodge Street
ⓒ 020 7299 1640
fopp.co.uk
⊕ 7/O6

**Offstage Theatre
& Film Bookshop**
34 Tavistock St, WC2
⊖ Covent Garden
ⓒ 020 7240 3883
offstagebooks.com
⊕ 7/Q9

Private screening rooms

195 Piccadilly
BAFTA, 195 Piccadilly, W1
⊜ Piccadilly Circus
℃ 020 7292 5800
bafta.org
⊕ 11/N10

Courthouse Hotel Kempinski
19-21 Great Marlborough St, W1
⊜ Oxford Circus
℃ 020 7297 5555
courthouse-hotel.com
⊕ 7/N8

One Aldwych
1 Aldgate, WC2
⊜ Temple
℃ 020 7300 1000
onealdwych.com
⊕ 7/R9

Covent Garden Hotel
10 Monmouth St, WC2
⊜ Covent Garden
℃ 020 7806 1000
firmdale.com
⊕ 7/P8

Haymarket Hotel
1 Suffolk Pl, SW1
⊜ Piccadilly Circus
℃ 020 7470 4000
firmdale.com
⊕ 11/P10

Rex Cinema & Bar
21 Rupert St, W1
⊜ Piccadilly Circus
℃ 020 7287 0102
rexbar.co.uk
⊕ 7/O9

Charlotte Street Hotel
15-17 Charlotte St, W1
⊜ Goodge Street
℃ 020 7806 2000
firmdale.com
⊕ 7/N6

The Mayfair
Stratton St, W1
⊜ Green Park
℃ 020 7629 7777
radissonedwardian.com
⊕ 11/M10

Soho Hotel
4 Richmond Mews, W1
⊜ Tottenham Court Rd
℃ 020 7559 3000
firmdale.com
⊕ 7/O8

06

See page 9 to scan the directory

07

DESIGNER HOTELS
AND ART ROOMS

Great Eastern Hotel
40 Liverpool Street, EC1

Previous page: One Aldwych
1 Aldwych, WC2

L ondon has some of the most creative and best designed hotels of anywhere in the world. So whether you like your hotel to march to a modern beat or reflect a bygone age, it's not hard to find a home away from home in a supremely artistic setting. The prospect of an Olympics-fuelled boom keeps hoteliers and interior designers on their mettle: each year brings a clutch of cutting-edge newcomers and superb revamps of grand old classics.

Contemporary art and design

Where style and boutique hotels are concerned, London has an embarrassment of riches. They might be small like the **Halkin** in Knightsbridge, or they might be as big as the **Great Eastern**, which reopened in the City in 2000 after a £70 million overhaul by Terence Conran. It's a vast style complex, its modern design tastefully attuned to the Victorian framework, and kitted out with wi-fi, DVD players in bedrooms, and no fewer than seven restaurants and bars. Bedrooms are chic throughout, from Frette linens via chocolate shag pile rugs to Eames chairs. The lobby serves as an exhibition space for modern art.

07

Boutique bouquet

In the world of London's boutique hotels, one name stands tall: Kit Kemp. With her husband Tim, the designer runs the small Firmdale chain, credited with bringing the English country house to the capital. Typical of the Kemp style is the **Charlotte Street Hotel**, which fuses classic English furnishings with avant-garde art and whose public rooms display art by Bloomsbury artists Vanessa Bell and Duncan Grant. Nearby the **Covent Garden Hotel** is handy for the Royal Opera House and West End theatres, with an A-list clientele, private screening room and wood-panelled library.

The **Soho Hotel** is rather different, a seriously hip urban hotel crafted from what was, of all things, a multi-level car park and done up with pinks and greens, modern furniture, art by British artists, and hi-tech facilities. The newest Firmdale treat is the **Haymarket Hotel**, open since May 2007 in the length of John Nash's colonnaded Suffolk Place.

It's a five-star hotel with swimming pool, individually designed rooms and suites, an exclusive four-storey townhouse, and a lobby decorated with paintings by John Virtue and a steel sculpture by Tony Cragg.

Another behemoth is the **Cumberland**. It has 900 rooms on its main site (another 119 a few metres away) and a massive lobby, sometimes compared to Tate Modern, featuring large-scale artworks and panels that change colour throughout the day. Big, too, are the flat-screen TVs in the rooms, which are minimalist in style but also, perhaps surprisingly, in dimensions.

Few hotels do modern design as carefully and impressively as the **St Martins Lane**, an Ian Schrager hotel designed by Philippe Starck. Among its attractions are the Light Bar, mood lighting options in the bedrooms, floor-to-ceiling windows and freestanding modern baths in limestone bathrooms. The Schrager/Starck combo's designer touch has also lent itself to the deluxe **Sanderson**, another sleek and thoroughly stylish design hotel that has a Salvador Dalí red lips sofa in the lobby, a purple lift and sleigh beds – panache all the way. Actors and musicians love the Long Bar and restaurant here.

07

Something a little different is the thrilling design of five-star **Baglioni**. Impeccably elegant – it's part of an Italian group, after all – it manages to be sober yet warm, with dark wood furniture and good use made of stripes on walls and beds. Sober yet warm also describes **One Aldwych**, in the heart of theatreland in a 1907 building that has been transformed by financier owner

The Hempel
31-35 Craven Hill Gardens, W2

Gordon Campbell Gray in collaboration with interior decorator Mary Fox Linton. It has a large contemporary art and sculpture collection, and there are original works of art in each room. Don't miss the 18-metre pool whose underwater fibre optics make it glitter.

Minimalist glamour

Ah yes, minimalism. The 'less is more' ethic took hold in the late 1980s with the opening of Anouska Hempel's influential **Blakes**, and still hasn't let go. Hempel's more recent hotel, **The Hempel**, takes minimalism to new levels of purity with dazzling, pristine white spaces that might be bleak were it not for the carefully feng shui-ed furniture and tactile fabrics, including linen, fake furs and suede. The bed in one of the suites is even spectacularly suspended from the ceiling.

The minimalist look has been so popular it even crops up in middle-range hotels. The **Southwark Rose**, for instance, clad with arty lobby decorated with smart photography and leather seating, has rooms done in dark woods and bright white linen and is perfectly located near the Globe theatre and Tate Modern.

Along the same lines is Clerkenwell's **The Zetter**, a loft hotel in a converted Victorian warehouse. It's all exposed brick and groovy 1970's designer furniture.

07

The Zetter
86 Clerkenwell Road, EC1

Rooms are airy with lots of pristeen white and neutral-tone woods jazzed up with wallpaper art, colour spot lighting and homely touches like old Penguin paperbacks. It won London's Best Small Hotel award in 2006.

Conran-designed **myhotel** in literary Bloomsbury is the hotel that propelled Asian fusion décor and feng shui into the minimalist London hotel scene. The rooms are white with stark black furniture, and there's a top floor suite with a private rooftop terrace and amazing views.

Artsy heritage

If you prefer your artistic accommodation trad rather than mod, you'll want something like the lovely 33-room **Rookery**, in a row of 18th century buildings in fashionable Clerkenwell between the West End and the City – very convenient for the Barbican and Tate Modern. Stay here and, if you squint a little so as to edit out the modern creature comforts like wireless internet, flat-screen TVs and sumptuous Egyptian cotton bedding, you'll feel like you've stepped into a novel by William Makepeace Thackeray or Alexandre Dumas. Polished wood panelling, stone floors, open fires, Gothic oak beds, claw-foot bathtubs and plaster busts are all part of the decor. Book the Rook's Nest, the substantial two-level suite, and you'll be treated to great views and a working Victorian bathing machine.

07

Brown's
33 Albemarle Street, W1

Arty for its guest list as much as the decor is Notting Hill's **Portobello Hotel**, a long-standing favourite with rock stars (Morrissey, Van Morrison, Alice Cooper), film stars (Gwyneth Paltrow, Natalie Portman, Colin Firth) and fashion types (Kate Moss, Naomi Campbell). Its rooms have old oil paintings, carved four-poster beds, long drapes, antique bathtubs and a smattering of Moroccan fittings and cushions. Another good Notting Hill address is **Guesthouse West**, a hip take on the B&B concept that has a changing art display in its retro lobby bar.

Literary heritage

Writers are a peripatetic lot, and thus habitual hotel users, enabling some hotels to accrue serious literary cachet. Only the faultlessly romantic **Cadogan** can offer its guests a room that saw one of the great dramas of literary history, the arrest of Oscar Wilde, which took place in what is now known as the Oscar Wilde Suite. It's done out in a style the old aesthete would surely have enjoyed, with sky blue walls, floor-to-ceiling silk curtains and bed covers bearing rich chocolate stripes. Oscar's friend, Lily Langtry, also stayed at the hotel in her capacity as mistress to King Edward VII.

Owner of another cast-iron literary pedigree is the wonderful **Hazlitt's**, in three Georgian townhouses at the heart of the city – one of which was home to the

07

Aristocratic icons

Claridge's, The Ritz, The Savoy, Brown's: these are London's hotel aristocrats – worldly, illustrious and sophisticated to their very doorknobs. Not that they're given to resting on laurels; **The Connaught** is just the latest to benefit from a multi-million pound transformation, adding a spa, 33 rooms and a design by Guy Oliver that keeps an understated British feel spiced with contemporary art and modern gizmos.

Artiest dame of the bunch is the West End's Savoy, built to accommodate audiences of the Gilbert & Sullivan shows next door. Its crea-tive guests have included George Gershwin, Sir Laurence Olivier and Vivien Leigh (who met when dining at the Savoy Grill), Lillian Gish, Marlene Dietrich and Whistler. Meanwhile, Monet painted the Thames from his window here. The art beat goes on with the Monet Suite Experience: two nights in one of the suites Monet painted in, a private guided tour of the National Gallery, four hours of art tuition and a supply of art materials. The Savoy also hosts such glamorous events as a Literary Cabaret Dinner hosted by The Savoy's writer in residence, Michael Morpurgo.

great 18th century essayist William Hazlitt. The food writer Anthony Bourdain has compared lodging here to "staying at a potty English uncle's when he's not at home" and you can see what he means. Old paintings, rugs, exquisitely carved oak beds, claw foot bathtubs, and some delightfully creaky rooms higher up all create a striking atmosphere. Web TVs lurk in antique cupboards, however, and the library boasts signed first editions from guests like Ted Hughes and JK Rowling. Staff are charming, too, so it's no wonder the hotel remains so popular with the film and media set.

The small but superbly equipped **22 Jermyn Street**, housed in a late 17th century building and a favourite with Thackeray, is ideal for a long stay as the 13 suites are like private apartments. After a hard day at the keyboard, guests can treat themselves on this elegant street renowned for men's requisites.

07

More bookish vibes, purloined from Arthur Conan Doyle's oeuvres, can be had at the **Sherlock Holmes**, which comes with the expected Holmesian paraphernalia of magnifying glasses and paintings of the detective and his colleague Dr Watson. The rooms appropriately look like groovy bachelor pads, and the lobby is a sleek affair of wood furniture and panelling.

Price indications are for a double room: £ up to £150; ££ from £151 to £250; £££ from £251 to £350; ££££ from £351 and over.

Contemporary art and design

Baglioni ££££
60 Hyde Park Gate, SW7
⊖ High St Kensington
℅ 020 7368 5700
baglionihotellondon.com
⊕ 9/F12

Cumberland ££
Great Cumberland Pl, W1
⊖ Marble Arch
℅ 020 7262 1234
guoman.com
⊕ 6/J8

Great Eastern £££
40 Liverpool St, EC2
⊖ Liverpool Street
℅ 020 7618 5000
great-eastern-hotel.co.uk
⊕ 8/Y7

Halkin ££££
5 Halkin St, SW1
⊖ Hyde Park Corner
℅ 020 7333 1000
halkin.como.bz
⊕ 10/L12

The Metropolitan ££££
19 Old Park Lane, W1
⊖ Hyde Park Corner
℅ 020 7447 1000
metropolitan.como.bz
⊕ 10/L11

One Aldwych £££
1 Aldwych, WC2
⊖ Temple
℅ 020 7300 1000
onealdwych.com
⊕ 7/R9

Sanderson £££
50 Berners St, W1
⊖ Oxford Circus
℅ 020 7300 1400
morganshotelgroup.com
⊕ 7/N7

St Martins Lane £££
45 St Martin's Lane, WC2
⊖ Leicester Square
℅ 020 7300 5500
stmartinslane.com
⊕ 7/P9

Trafalgar £££
2 Spring Gdns, SW1
⊖ Charing Cross
℅ 020 7870 2900
hilton.co.uk/trafalgar
⊕ 11/P10

Minimalist glamour

Blakes £££
33 Roland Gdns, SW7
⊖ Gloucester Road
℅ 020 7370 6701
blakeshotels.com
⊕ 13/F15

The Hempel £££
31 Craven Hill Gdns, W2
⊖ Lancaster Gate
℅ 020 7298 9000
the-hempel.co.uk
⊕ 5/F9

Myhotel Bloomsbury ££
11-13 Bayley St, WC1
⊖ Goodge Street
℅ 020 7667 6000
myhotels.co.uk
⊕ 7/O7

Myhotel Chelsea ££
35 Ixworth Pl, SW3
⊖ South Kensington
℅ 020 7225 7500
myhotels.co.uk
⊕ 14/H15

Southwark Rose ££
47 Southwark Bridge
Rd, SE1
⊖ London Bridge
℅ 020 7015 1480
southwarkrosehotel.co.uk
⊕ 12/V11

The Zetter ££
86 Clerkenwell Rd, EC1
⊖ Farringdon
℅ 020 7324 4444
thezetter.com
⊕ 8/T6

Artsy heritage

The Gore ££
189 Queen's Gate, SW7
⊖ South Kensington
☎ 020 7584 6601
gorehotel.com
⊕ 9/F13

The Lanesborough ££££
Hyde Park Corner, W1
⊖ Hyde Park Corner
☎ 020 7259 5599
lanesborough.com
⊕ 10/K12

Portobello Hotel ££
22 Stanley Gdns, W11
⊖ Holland Park
☎ 020 7727 2777
portobello-hotel.co.uk
⊕ 5/B9

Guesthouse West ££
163-165 Westbourne
Grove, W11
⊖ Notting Hill Gate
☎ 020 7792 9800
guesthousewest.com
⊕ 5/C8

Miller's Residence £
111a Westbourne
Grove, W2
⊖ Notting Hill Gate
☎ 020 7243 1024
millersuk.com
⊕ 5/C8

The Rookery ££
12 Peter's Lane, EC1
⊖ Farringdon
☎ 020 7336 0931
rookeryhotel.com
⊕ 8/U6

Boutique bouquet

07

Charlotte Street Hotel ££
15-17 Charlotte St, W1
⊖ Goodge Street
☎ 020 7806 2000
firmdale.com
⊕ 7/N6

Haymarket Hotel £££
1 Suffolk Pl, SW1
⊖ Piccadilly Circus
☎ 020 7470 4000
firmdale.com
⊕ 11/P10

Pelham Hotel ££
15 Cromwell Pl, SW7
⊖ South Kensington
☎ 020 7589 8288
firmdale.com
⊕ 13/G14

Covent Garden Hotel £££
10 Monmouth St, WC2
⊖ Covent Garden
☎ 020 7806 1000
firmdale.com
⊕ 7/P8

Number Sixteen ££
16 Sumner Pl, SW7
⊖ South Kensington
☎ 020 7589 5232
firmdale.com
⊕ 13-14/G15

Soho Hotel £££
4 Richmond Mews, W1
⊖ Tottenham Court Rd
☎ 020 7559 3000
firmdale.com
⊕ 7/O8

The Ritz
150 Piccadilly, W1

Aristocratic icons

Berkeley ££££
Wilton Pl, SW1
⊖ Hyde Park Corner
© 020 7235 6000
theberkeleyhotellondon.com
⊕ 10/K12

Claridge's £££
55 Brook St, W1
⊖ Bond Street
© 020 7629 8860
claridges.co.uk
⊕ 6/H9

Ritz ££££
150 Piccadilly, W1
⊖ Green Park
© 020 7493 8181
theritzlondon.com
⊕ 11/M11

Brown's £££
33 Albemarle St, W1
⊖ Green Park
© 020 7493 6020
roccofortehotels.com
⊕ 11/M10

Connaught ££££
Carlos Pl, W1
⊖ Bond Street
the-connaught.co.uk
⊕ 6/L9

Savoy £££
The Strand, WC2
⊖ Embankment
© 020 7836 4343
savoy-group.co.uk
⊕ 11/Q10

Literary heritage

22 Jermyn Street £££
22 Jermyn St, SW1
⊖ Picadilly Circus
© 020 7734 2353
22jermyn.com
⊕ 11/N10

Dukes £££
St James's Place, SW1
⊖ Green Park
© 020 7491 4840
dukeshotel.com
⊕ 11/N11

**Sherlock Holmes
Hotel** £
108 Baker St, W1
⊖ Baker Street
© 020 7486 6161
sherlockholmeshotel.com
⊕ 6/K6

07

Cadogan £££
75 Sloane St, SW1
⊖ Sloane Square
© 020 7235 7141
steinhotels.com/cadogan
⊕ 14/J14

Hazlitt's ££
6 Frith St, W1
⊖ Tottenham Court Rd
© 020 7434 1771
hazlittshotel.com
⊕ 7/O8

See page 9
to scan the
directory

08

RESTAURANTS,
CAFES AND BARS

National Dining Rooms
National Gallery, WC2

Previous page: Rex Whistler Restaurant
at Tate Britain, SW1

L ondon's high-end restaurant scene is alive and thriving, so much so that the *Guardian* coined the city nothing less than "the culinary capital of the world" not so long ago. The very thought is enough to whet your appetite. And since cooking is now ranked as one of the arts, it's hardly surprising to learn that where there's cultural excellence, culinary excellence is usually just a step away.

Museum restaurants

Gone is the time when museum canteens served institutional cuppas, tired sandwiches and slabs of leathery lasagne. These days the typical refreshment stop at a big London collection is designer styled, welcoming and attuned to the tastes of a discerning clientele.

08

Some museum restaurants are now even seen as destination venues in their own right. Among these is the sleek **Blueprint Café** at the Design Museum with its breathtaking view of the Thames, and **Café Bagatelle**, in a glass-roofed courtyard at the Wallace Collection. Tea among the Corinthian columns of **Queen Anne's Orangery** at Kensington Palace is another experience well worth the trip.

For sustenance more substantial than teas, the new **National Dining Rooms** at the National Gallery is a terrific addition to the city's cultural eating spots, and offers excellent British food like sea trout with English asparagus, heritage tomato salad, English cheeses, raised pork pie, ales and ciders. More à la carte British food is served in the **Portrait Restaurant** on the top floor of the National Portrait Gallery. Here, dishes like saddle of rabbit with black pudding and bacon roll or confit fillet of wild seabass are set off nicely by the spectacular rooftop view. Not to be outdone, Tate Britain's commendable **Rex Whistler Restaurant** dishes up superb European fusion fare in a dining room decorated with Rex Whistler's jolly mural *In Pursuit of Rare Meats*.

Art land haunts

The prime art gallery territory of Cork Street and New Bond Street overlaps with some first rate dining. The five-space venue **Sketch** is glamorous and fashionable, if notoriously costly. There, choose between the Lecture Room for Pierre Gagnaire's sumptuous cuisine, the less expensive Gallery, light lunch venue the Glade, the Parlour for patisseries or East for cocktails

Smaller and more relaxed, **Patterson's** is a father-and-son restaurant that manages to be both chic and unstuffy, and whose delicious fusion food is prepared and served with conspicuous care. A short stroll away, the new **Via Condotti** is the latest arena for the talents of chef Pasquale Amico, who rustles up superb regional Italian food at great prices. The wine list is good, too. There's more decent Italian at Conran restaurant **Sartoria**, which has a distinctly Milanese vibe, and the supremely authentic and stylish **Alloro** wins hands down for refined and faultlessly precise cooking.

With loving attention to the tableware and the arrangement of colours and patterns in the food itself, the best Japanese cuisine often looks like a work of art, which is perhaps why Nobu opened its third London outpost, **Nobu Berkeley**, in art land. There's a great bar on the ground floor, and the restaurant upstairs serves exquisitely fresh seared tuna and an unusual take on scallop sashimi, drizzled with oil and topped with chives. **Umu** is another top-flight Japanese venue which focuses on the ultra-refined cuisine of Kyoto and benefits from especially charming staff.

08

More old-fashioned surroundings can be enjoyed at the **Wolseley**, a restaurant in the grand European tradition, complete with marble floor, grand pillars and arches. Housed in a building that was put up to showcase Wolseley cars in the 1920's, it's one of the most attractive settings for a meal anywhere in the

Rules
35 Maiden Lane, WC2

city and popular with staff from the nearby Condé Nast offices. If that's not quite swish enough, there's always the **Ritz**, perhaps for afternoon tea, or Mayfair institution **Langan's Brasserie**, where there's art on the menu, literally; it was designed by Hockney.

Finally, out east you'll find Farringdon's elite bastion of British cuisine, **St John,** which heaves with the art crowd at the time of the Frieze Art Fair. Nose-to-tail eating is the motto here, so plenty of unusual meaty offerings are on the menu.

Theatre and literary dens

The celebrated **Ivy** is probably the most famous thespian gathering ground after the Groucho (and the Groucho is members only) and has been frequented by almost every actor who has ever worked in London, from Noel Coward to the latest Doctor Who. You can even expect to see literary luminaries of the wattage of Harold Pinter at its tables.

08

Under the same owners, London's best known fish restaurant **J Sheekey** is another West End venue that's been popular with theatre actors and writers for decades (it opened in 1896). Don't miss the house special, Cornish fish stew. Even more venerable than Sheekey's is **Rules**, the oldest restaurant in London.

Overnight sensations

Many of the stylish hotels discussed in Chapter Seven have excellent restaurants offering cuisine by some of the country's top chefs. Bring supremely creative cooking to arty surroundings, and arty and creative diners will come flocking. The Gordon Ramsay empire includes his own kitchen, **Gordon Ramsay at Claridge's,** and the kitchens of two of his viceroys, Marcus Wareing and Angela Hartnett, who preside over the restaurants **Petrus** at the Berkeley and **Angela Hartnett** at the **Connaught** respectively.

All three serve food at the very pinnacle of culinary achievement and conse-quently all three require you to make your booking eight or nine weeks in advance.

Less exclusive, though still eminent in its field, is **The Grill,** a new addition to Brown's Hotel that's steered by executive chef Laurence Glayzer, formerly of the Savoy Grill. Food here, as you would expect from the setting, is wonderfully traditional, lots of beef (rib, rump, Rossini), Morecambe Bay potted shrimps, pudding served with custard and a decent wine list.

Refuel at the Soho Hotel is more cosmopolitan and innovative. The car references allude to the hotel's former function as a car park.

The restaurant was founded in 1798, and its literary patrons have included Dickens, Thackeray, Galsworthy and HG Wells. Not content with merely dining there, many novelists, Evelyn Waugh, Graham Greene and John Le Carré among them, have written the restaurant, famous for its game dishes, into their books.

The London publishing world still has its heartland in Bloomsbury and Soho, and rubbing shoulders with bookish types over lunch or dinner is a common experience in Soho, though not in Bloomsbury, which has rather a dearth of places to eat. When publishers have a bestseller on their hands, they celebrate at **L'Escargot**, a Marco Pierre White kitchen that has two lovely dining rooms, a high-class brasserie space on the ground floor and the Picasso Room on the first floor. For more workaday power lunches, they congregate in venues like the airy, prize-winning David Chipperfield-designed **Circus** – a buzzy, tastefully redecorated purveyor of good modern French cuisine that packs in a mix of smart businessmen and artistic bookland types.

New arrival on the block is **Arbutus**, unremarkable enough to look at but a standout for the quality and value of its Euro fusion menu. Dishes like salad with fresh sheep's ricotta and summer vegetables or a squid and mackerel burger served with barbecue sauce are top notch.

08

Gordon Ramsay at Claridge's
Brook St, W1

Fashionista favourites

Mayfair, Knightsbridge and Kensington, havens for shopping savvy Londoners, are stuffed with restaurants almost as glam and shiny as a new Hermès bag. Since it opened in 2005, **Galvin Bistrot de Luxe** has been the talk of the modish masses and dedicated followers of food fashion alike. Brothers Chris and Jeff Galvin preside in the kitchen, turning out dishes like velouté of asparagus with poached duck egg that consistently wow the local ladies who lunch.

Sotheby's Café inside the famous auction house is another genteel spot popular with both ladies who lunch and impeccably dressed young gents from the local galleries. Decorated with dark woods and smart black-and-white photos, it serves pleasant, straightforward light meals.

Amaya is exactly the sort of Indian restaurant you'd expect to find in Knightsbridge. Beautifully kitted out with rosewood panels, chandeliers and earthenware trinkets, it serves first-class biriyanis and kebabs. **Zuma** enjoyed blanket coverage from all the stylish parts of the press when it opened some years before Amaya, but remains just as glamorous today. Not only do the rotobaki grill, sushi bar and main dining area look of-the-moment, but the Japanese food is terrific and the sake selection at the bar overwhelming.

08

Museum restaurants

Blueprint Café
Design Museum, Shad
Thames, SE1
⊖ London Bridge
ⓒ 020 7378 7031
danddlondon.com
⊕ 12/Z11

Café Bagatelle
Wallace Collection,
Manchester Sq, W1
⊖ Bond Street
ⓒ 020 7935 0687
wallacecollection.org
⊕ 6/K7

National Dining Rooms
National Gallery, WC2
⊖ Charing Cross
ⓒ 020 7747 2885
nationalgallery.org.uk
⊕ 11/P10

Portrait Restaurant
National Portrait Gallery,
WC2
⊖ Charing Cross
ⓒ 020 7306 0055
npg.org.uk
⊕ 11/P10

Queen Anne's Orangery
Kensington Palace, W8
⊖ Queensway
ⓒ 020 7937 9561
hrp.org.uk
⊕ 9/E11

The Rex Whistler
Restaurant
Tate Britain, Millbank, SW1
⊖ Pimlico
ⓒ 020 7887 8000
tate.org.uk
⊕ 15/P16

The Ritz
150 Piccadilly, W1
⊖ Green Park
ⓒ 020 7493 8181
theritzhotel.co.uk
⊕ 11/M11

Rocket
4-6 Lancashire Court, W1
⊖ Bond Street
ⓒ 020 7629 2889
rocketrestaurants.co.uk
⊕ 6/M9

Sartoria
20 Savile Row, W1
⊖ Oxford Circus
ⓒ 020 7534 7000
conran.com
⊕ 6-7/N9

Sketch
9 Conduit St, W1
⊖ Oxford Circus
ⓒ 0870 777 4488
sketch.uk.com
⊕ 6/M9

The Square
6-10 Bruton St, W1
⊖ Bond Street
ⓒ 020 7495 7100
squarerestaurant.com
⊕ 6/M9

St John
26 St John St, EC1
⊖ Farringdon
ⓒ 020 7251 0848
stjohnrestaurant.co.uk
⊕ 4/T4

Umu
14-16 Bruton Pl, W1
⊖ Bond Street
ⓒ 020 7499 8881
umurestaurant.com
⊕ 6/M9

Via Condotti
23 Conduit St, W1
⊖ Oxford Circus
ⓒ 020 7493 7050
⊕ 6/M9

The Wolseley
160 Piccadilly, W1
⊖ Green Park
ⓒ 020 7499 6996
thewolseley.com
⊕ 11/M11

Theatre and literary dens

Andrew Edmunds
46 Lexington St, W1
⊖ Piccadilly Circus
☎ 020 7437 5708
⊕ 7/O9

J Sheekey
32 St Martin's Court, WC2
⊖ Leicester Square
☎ 020 7240 2565
j-sheekey.co.uk
⊕ 7/P9

Oriel Brasserie
50-51 Sloane Sq, SW1
⊖ Sloane Square
☎ 020 7730 4275
⊕ 14/K14

Arbutus
63-64 Frith St, W1
⊖ Tottenham Court Rd
☎ 020 7734 4545
arbutusrestaurant.co.uk
⊕ 7/O8

Joe Allen
13 Exeter St, WC2
⊖ Covent Garden
☎ 020 7836 0651
joeallenrestaurant.com
⊕ 7/R9

Racine
239 Brompton Road, SW3
⊖ Knightsbridge
☎ 020 7584 4477
⊕ 10/I13

Circus
1 Upper James St, W1
⊖ Piccadilly Circus
☎ 020 7534 4000
egami.co.uk
⊕ 6-7/N9

L'Escargot
48 Greek St, W1
⊖ Leicester Square
☎ 020 7437 2679
whitestarline.org.uk
⊕ 7/P8

Rules
35 Maiden Lane, WC2
⊖ Covent Garden
☎ 020 7836 5341
rules.co.uk
⊕ 7/Q9

The Ivy
1 West St, WC2
⊖ Leicester Square
☎ 020 7836 4751
the-ivy.co.uk
⊕ 7/P9

La Trouvaille
12A Newburgh St, W1
⊖ Oxford Circus
☎ 020 7287 8488
latrouvaille.co.uk
⊕ 7/N8

Zilli Fish
36-40 Brewer St, W1
⊖ Piccadilly Circus
☎ 020 7734 8649
zillialdo.com
⊕ 7/O9

08

St. JOHN

Art land haunts

Alloro
19-20 Dover St, W1
⊖ Green Park
ⓒ 020 7495 4768
alloro-restaurant.co.uk
⊕ 11/M10

Giardinetto
39-40 Albemarle St, W1
⊖ Green Park
ⓒ 020 7493 7091
giardinetto.co.uk
⊕ 11/M10

Langan's Brasserie
Stratton St, W1
⊖ Green Park
ⓒ 020 7491 8822
langansrestaurants.com
⊕ 11/M10

Mirabelle
56 Curzon St, W1
⊖ Green Park
ⓒ 020 7499 4636
whitestarline.org.uk
⊕ 10/L11

Nobu Berkeley
15 Berkeley St, W1
⊖ Green Park
ⓒ 020 7290 9222
noburestaurants.com
⊕ 11/M10

Patterson's
4 Mill St, W1
⊖ Bond Street
ⓒ 020 7499 1308
pattersonsrestaurant.co.uk
⊕ 6/M9

Overnight sensations

**Angela Hartnett at
the Connaught**
16 Carlos Pl, W1
⊖ Bond Street
ⓒ 020 7592 1222
gordonramsay.com
⊕ 6/L9

The Dining Room
The Goring, 17 Beeston
Pl, SW1
⊖ Victoria
ⓒ 020 7396 9000
goringhotel.co.uk
⊕ 11/M13

The Grill
Brown's Hotel,
33 Albemarle St, W1
⊖ Green Park
ⓒ 020 7493 6020
roccofortehotels.com
⊕ 11/M10

**Gordon Ramsay
at Claridge's**
Claridge's, Brook St, W1
⊖ Bond St
ⓒ 020 7499 0099
gordonramsay.com
⊕ 6/L9

Petrus
The Berkeley, Wilton Pl,
SW1
⊖ Hyde Park Corner
ⓒ 020 7235 1200
marcuswareing.com
⊕ 10/K12

Refuel
Soho Hotel, 4 Richmond
Mews, W1
⊖ Tottenham Court Rd
ⓒ 020 7559 3007
refuelsoho.com
⊕ 7/O8

Fashionista favourites

Amaya
Motcomb St, SW1
🚇 Knightsbridge
📞 020 7823 1166
realindianfood.com
🕑 10/K13

Galvin Bistrot de Luxe
66 Baker St, W1
🚇 Baker Street
📞 020 7935 4007
galvinbistrotdeluxe.co.uk
🕑 6/K6

Tom's Kitchen
27 Cale St, SW3
🚇 South Kensington
📞 020 7349 0202
www.tomskitchen.co.uk
🕑 14/H15

The Boxwood Café
The Berkeley, Wilton Pl,
SW1
🚇 Hyde Park Corner
📞 020 7235 1010
gordonramsay.com
🕑 10/K12

Nicole's
158 New Bond St, W1
🚇 Bond Street
📞 020 7499 8408
nicolefarhi.com
🕑 6/M8

Zafferano
15 Lowndes St, SW1
🚇 Knightsbridge
📞 020 7235 5800
🕑 10/K13

Cecconi's
5a Burlington Gdns, W1
🚇 Piccadilly Circus
📞 020 7434 1500
cecconis.co.uk
🕑 11/N10

Sotheby's Café
34-35 New Bond St, W1
🚇 Bond Street
📞 020 7293 5077
sothebys.com
🕑 6/M8

The Zetter
86-88 Clerkenwell Rd,
EC1
🚇 Farringdon
📞 020 7324 4455
thezetter.com
🕑 8/T6

08

Daphne's
112 Draycott Av, SW3
🚇 South Kensington
📞 020 7589 4257
daphnes-restaurant.co.uk
🕑 14/I15

Tom Aikens
43 Elystan St, SW3
🚇 South Kensington
📞 020 7584 2003
tomaikens.co.uk
🕑 14/I15

Zuma
5 Raphael St, SW7
🚇 Knightsbridge
📞 020 7584 1010
zumarestaurant.com
🕑 10/I12

See page 9
to scan the
directory

09

FESTIVALS, FAIRS
AND HAPPENINGS

London Film Festival
BFI Southbank, SE1

Previous page: Royal Albert Hall
Kensington Gore, SW7

L ondon's arts calendar is bursting at the seams. You could attend an arty happening every day of the week and still only scratch the surface. The focus of any given function might be local or international, a single art form or several, the duration a day, a week, a month or longer. This chapter can only hope to highlight a few of the more representative creative celebrations; for others, consult local listings publications.

Art bonanza

The annual **Turner Prize** is the art story most covered in the non-arts media, and its entrants are exhibited at Tate Britain in the autumn. The larger and more important **Frieze Art Fair** goes relatively unremarked in the national press. Such is the newspaper appeal of a big money prize. Non-competitive Frieze presents a stellar line-up of modern artists and international exhibitors and is one of the modern art world's biggest events, run concurrently with the **Zoo Art Fair**. A little more wide-ranging in scope since it includes works from the early 20th century, the giant **London Art Fair** sells pieces by anyone from Lowry to Banksy. It celebrates its 20th anniversary in 2008, and since 2007

09

has included a photography section, Photo50. The largest entirely photographic event is **PhotoLondon**, held by the river at Old Billingsgate in June.

Other opportunities for private buyers include the **Affordable Art Fair** in Battersea Park in March, while Brick Lane's **Free Range** offers an array of art by final-year art students from across London. Recent graduates also exhibit, of course, at the various art schools' summer shows. Look out, too, for **Collect** at the Victoria & Albert Museum in January, the only international art fair in Europe that zeroes in on contemporary applied and decorative arts, in particular from the UK and the Netherlands.

The most popular annual event is the **Royal Academy Summer Exhibition**, the world's largest open-entry contemporary art show. Every summer for 200 years it has shown work by unknown and rising artists, alongside that of more established names. Around 9,000 paintings, sculptures, photographs, drawings, prints and architectural models are entered each year.

Architecture and design

Architecture fans should aim to be here during **Architecture Week** in June, when the art of the building designer is celebrated in a mass of screenings, talks, walks, building tours, exhibitions, excavations and children's activities; or in September, when some of the city's most illustrious buildings open their doors to the public for **Open House London**. There's also the **Serpentine Gallery**'s highbrow Summer Pavilion, with a lively schedule of talks and film screenings held in a purpose-built temporary pavilion commissioned from a different international architect each year.

For design buffs, the big calendar event is the **London Design Festival** in September. As many as 300,000 people come to view the hottest new furniture, graphics and architecture in more than 150 venues around the city, often grouped around a major cultural hub like the Southbank Centre.

Film festivals

More than 50 film festivals take place in London every year. The leader of the pack and the largest public film event in the country, is the **London Film Festival**, held every October since 1957, bringing in big-name actors and filmmakers from all over the world, and screens around 180 new films, British and international, principally at BFI Southbank and Odeon West End.

Other film festivals have a special focus. The **Human Rights Watch International Film Festival** addresses social topics via documentaries and fiction.

09

Dance Umbrella
Various venues

Raindance is an indie film haven held in October, while **onedotzero**, **Resfest**, **Halloween Short Film Festival** and **Rushes Soho Shorts Festival** over the burgeoning world of short films.

Music extravaganzas

The Proms, officially known as the **BBC Sir Henry Wood Promenade Concerts** are one of London's best-loved and most emblematic artistic events. The festival of orchestral music at the Royal Albert Hall has been an institution since 1895, and the annual line-up runs to 70 concerts with a repertoire of anything from Beethoven to Pärt. The name comes from the seatless promenade area in front of the stage; the festival is unusual in that the cheapest tickets give access to the best positions. If you want to attend the notoriously kitsch Last Night, you need to have bought tickets to several other concerts during the festival.

The counterweight to the Proms' exclusively orchestral focus is the excellent **City of London Festival**, where chamber music is performed in the beautiful halls of ancient livery companies, hidden down small streets and normally closed to the public. Just before the CLF is the **Spitalfields Festival** with a baroque and early music flavour and is renowned for performing work by lesser-known composers as well as the greats.

09

Open air events

London doesn't have the climatic reliability of Avignon or Barcelona, but there are plenty of cultural showcases willing to take the risk of a summer shower. The annual **Trafalgar Square Festival** in August encompassing gigs, dance, street theatre and more is the most centrally located, while there are concerts of popular classical music as part of the summertime **Picnic Concerts** at Hampstead's Kenwood House and at Marble Hill House in Twickenham. The ten-week **Opera Holland Park** festival puts up a special temporary theatre in Holland Park, whose boards see a handful of productions following each other in quick succession. Jazz enthusiasts can savour the sounds of various mainstream performers at five evening concerts in Walpole Park during the July **Ealing Jazz Festival**, and films are screened at an ever-increasing spread of open-air spaces including Hyde Park, Kensington Gardens, Trafalgar Square, and at the Scoop amphitheatre in front of City Hall (**More Movies**). Probably the finest outdoor setting for cinema is the main courtyard at Somerset House during the **Film4 Summer Screen** season.

In addition to these headlining events, the **Barbican Centre, Southbank Centre** and **Wigmore Hall** stage a variety of themed classical seasons throughout the year.

Rock and pop festivals are usually held in the open air and jazz likewise, though the biggest jazz event, the **London Jazz Festival**, is an indoor affair. This ten-day jamboree takes over a long list of venues, and attracts some of the world's top performers. More intimate and more local is the **Riverfront Jazz Festival**, a five-day rundown of gigs in cafés and pubs in Greenwich.

Theatre and dance

Theatre festivals, as opposed to the forest of individual theatrical productions, are thin on the ground, but this numerical shortage is almost cancelled out by the sheer heft of the all-year long **Barbican International Theatre Events** (acronymically known as BITE), which pulls in a vast range of off-beat and exotic shows from all over the world during its annual six-month run. Theatre and live shows are its main pillars and some performers come from as far afield as Cambodia. Political and social upheaval are recurring themes. Productions have included *Weyreap's Battle,* performed by dancers who survived the Khmer Rouge, Peter Brook's version of *Sizwe Bansi is Dead*, and a production of Shakespeare's *Coriolanus* in Japanese directed by Yukio Ninagawa.

09

Courtauld Institute of Art
Somerset House, Strand, WC2

Dance has several festivals to its credit, including one of the world's best, **Dance Umbrella** in October dedicated purely to contemporary dance. As at the Proms, the stalls are taken out for the duration of the festival, providing space for 500 members of the audience to see the action right up close. **Big Dance**, in July, is a self-proclaimed celebration of the joy of dance. Its lively schedule of street performances, gigs, classes, and disciplines range from ballet and Bollywood to lambada and lindy hop to ceroc and capoeira.

A different sort of physical expression is honoured by the **London International Mime Festival** in January – a fortnight's worth of inventive and unusual mime art by performers from home and abroad. It's also a forum for avant-garde puppetry, of which British troupe Faulty Optic is one of the more striking exponents. More puppetry can be seen at the **May Fayre & Puppet Festival** in Covent Garden – some of whose puppets are as large as the puppeteers.

09

There are many locally based but world-encompassing events, too, that whip up heady cocktails of jugglers, clowns, stuntmen, latter-day mummers, thesps and giant works of art, for events like the **Greenwich & Docklands International Festival**, the **Brick Lane Festival** and, of course, the **Notting Hill Carnival.**

Art bonanza

Affordable Art Fair
Mid March
Battersea Park, SW11
🚉 Battersea Park
📞 020 8246 4848
affordableartfair.co.uk
⊕ Off map

Chelsea College of Art and Design
May and June
16 John Islip St, SW1
🚇 Pimlico
📞 020 7514 7751
chelsea.arts.ac.uk
⊕ 15/P16

Collect
Late January
V&A, Cromwell Rd, SW7
🚇 South Kensington
📞 020 7278 7700
craftscouncil.org.
uk/collect
⊕ 13/F14

Free Range
June
Various locations, Brick
Lane, E1
free-range.org.uk

Frieze Art Fair
Mid October
Regent's Park, NW1
🚇 Regent's Park
📞 020 7833 7270
friezeartfair.com
⊕ 2/K3

London Art Fair
Mid January
BDC, 52 Upper St, N1
🚇 Angel
📞 020 7288 6736
londonartfair.co.uk
⊕ 4/T2

Photo-London
Early June
1 Old Billingsgate
Walk, EC3
🚇 Monument
📞 020 7283 2800
photo-london.com
⊕ 12/X9

Royal Academy Summer Exhibition
June-August
Piccadilly, W1
🚇 Piccadilly Circus
📞 020 7300 8000
royalacademy.org.uk
⊕ 11/M11

Royal College of Art Summer Show
May-July
Kensington Gore, SW7
🚇 Gloucester Rd
📞 020 7590 4444
rca.ac.uk
⊕ 9-10/G12

ScopeLondon
Mid October
Regent's Park, NW1
🚇 Regent's Park
scope-art.com
⊕ 2/K3

Turner Prize
October-January
Tate Britain, Millbank, SW1
🚇 Pimlico
📞 020 7887 8000
tate.org.uk
⊕ 15/P16

Zoo Art Fair
October
Regent's Park, NW1
🚇 Regent's Park
📞 020 8964 3272
zooartfair.com
⊕ 2/K3

Music extravaganzas

Barbican Centre
Silk St, EC2
🚇 Barbican
📞 020 7638 8891
barbican.org.uk
✪ 8/W6

Hampstead Highgate Festival
Mid May
Various venues in
Hampstead and
Highgate
📞 020 7391 9241
hamandhighfest.co.uk

Spitalfields Festival
June
Christ Church
Spitalfields, Commercial
St, E1
🚇 Liverpool St
📞 020 7377 1362
spitalfieldsfestival.org.uk
✪ 8/Y6

BBC Sir Henry Wood Promenade Concerts
July-September
Royal Albert Hall,
Kensington Gore, SW7
🚇 Gloucester Rd
📞 020 7589 8212
bbc.co.uk/proms
✪ 9-10/G12

London Jazz Festival
November
Various venues
📞 020 7324 1880
serious.org.uk

Southbank Centre
Belvedere Road, SE1
🚇 Waterloo
southbankcentre.co.uk
✪ 11/R11

City of London Festival
Late June-mid July
Various venues in the City
📞 020 7796 4949
colf.org

Rhythm Sticks
July
Southbank Centre, SE1
🚇 Waterloo
📞 020 7921 0973
southbankcentre.co.uk
✪ 11/S10

Wigmore Hall
36 Wigmore St, W1
🚇 Bond Street
📞 020 7935 2141
wigmore-hall.org.uk
✪ 6/K8

Coin Street Festival
June-August
Bernie Spain Gdns,
South Bank, SE1
🚇 Waterloo
📞 020 7401 3610
coinstreet.org
✪ 11/S10

Riverfront Jazz Festival
Late September
Various venues in
Greenwich
🚇 Cutty Sark
📞 020 8921 4456
riverfrontjazz.co.uk
✪ Off map

09

Film

Black Filmmaker International Film Festival
September
Various venues
℡ 020 8531 9199
bfmmedia.com

Halloween Short Film Festival *January*
ICA, The Mall, SW1
⊖ Piccadilly Circus
℡ 020 7766 1407
shortfilms.org.uk
⊕ 11/O11

Human Rights Watch International Film Festival *Late March*
Various venues
℡ 020 7713 2773
hrw.org/iff

London Film Festival
October-November
BFI Southbank, SE1
⊖ Waterloo
℡ 020 7928 3535
lff.org.uk
⊕ 11/S10

onedotzero
May-June
ICA, The Mall, SW1
⊖ Trafalgar Sq
℡ 020 7766 1407
onedotzero.com
⊕ 11/O11

Portobello Film Festival
August
Various venues on
Portobello Rd, W10
℡ 020 8960 0996
portobellofilmfestival.com
⊕ 5/A6

Raindance
October
Various cinemas on
Shaftesbury Av
⊖ Leicester Sq
℡ 020 7287 3833
raindance.co.uk
⊕ 7/O9

Resfest
September-October
BFI Southbank, SE1
⊖ Waterloo
℡ 020 7928 3232
resfest.com
⊕ 11/S10

Rushes Soho Shorts Festival
Late July
Various venues in Soho
sohoshorts.com

Theatre and dance

Barbican International Theatre Events (BITE)
January-June
Silk St, EC2
⊖ Barbican
℡ 020 7638 8891
barbican.org.uk
⊕ 8/W6

Dance Umbrella
September and October
Various venues
℡ 020 8741 4040
danceumbrella.co.uk

May Fayre & Puppet Festival *mid May*
St Paul's Church Gdn,
Bedford St, WC2
⊖ Covent Gdn
℡ 020 7375 0441
alternativearts.co.uk
⊕ 7/Q9

Big Dance
Mid July
Various venues
℡ 020 7983 4000
london.gov.uk/bigdance

Greenwich & Docklands International Festival
July Various venues in Greenwich&Docklands
℡ 020 8305 1818
festival.org

Notting Hill Carnival
Various venues in Notting Hill
⊖ Notting Hill Gate
lnhc.org.uk
⊕ 9/C10

Brick Lane Festival
Second Sunday in September
Brick Lane & Allen Gdns, E1
⊖ Aldgate East
℡ 020 7655 0906
bricklanefestival.com
⊕ 8/Z6

London International Mime Festival
Second half of January
Various venues
℡ 020 7637 5661
mimefest.co.uk

Watch This Space National Theatre
June-August
Southbank Centre, SE1
⊖ Waterloo
℡ 020 7452 3400
nationaltheatre.org.uk
⊕ 11/S10

Architecture and design

100% Design
Earls Court 2, SW5
⊖ Earls Court
100percentdesign.co.uk
⊕ 13/D15

Decorex
Royal Hospital Rd, SW3
⊖ Sloane Square
℡ 020 7833 3373
decorex.com
⊕ 14/J16

Open House London
Various venues
℡ 020 7383 2131
openhouselondon.org

Architecture Week
Various venues
℡ 020 7973 5246
architectureweek.co.uk

London Design Festival
Various venues
℡ 020 7739 3814
londondesignfestival.com

Serpentine Gallery
Kensington Gdns, W2
⊖ South Kensington
℡ 020 7402 6075
serpentinegallery.org
⊕ 9/B13

09

Open air events

Ealing Jazz Festival
Walpole Park, W5
⊖ Ealing Broadway
ⓣ 020 8825 6640
ealing.gov.uk
⊕ Off map

Film 4 Summer Screen
Somerset House,
Strand, WC2
⊖ Temple
ⓣ 020 7845 4671
somersethousesummer.
org.uk
⊕ 11/R9

More Movies
The Scoop, The Queen's
Walk, SE1
⊖ London Bridge
morelondon.co.uk/scoop
⊕ 12/X11

Opera Holland Park
Holland Park, W8
⊖ Holland Park
ⓣ 020 7361 3570
operahollandpark.com
⊕ 9/B11

Picnic Concerts
Marble Hill, Richmond
Rd, Twickenham
⊛ St Margarets
ⓣ 020 8892 5115
picnicconcerts.com
⊕ Off map

Trafalgar Square Festival
Trafalgar Sq, WC1
⊖ Charing Cross
london.gov.uk/
trafalgarsquare
⊕ 11/P10

The London Design Festival
Various venues

09

See page 9
to scan the
directory

VENI, VIDI, VICI

Goldsmiths
New Cross, SE14

Previous page: Courtauld Institute of Art
Somerset House, Strand, WC2

Whether you've felt the prickle of London's creative electricity at first hand or just vicariously in the pages of this book, the temptation to join and contribute to the city's cultural scene will always be strong, and London is well set up to feed the artist in you. The roster of arts and ways to pursue them is dizzying -- beginners, full-time, part-time, short courses and evening classes; government-funded or privately run. Multi-disciplinary universities and world-famous conservatories of the quality of the Royal Academy of Dramatic Art (RADA), Goldsmiths and the Slade School of Fine Art are all based in central London.

If there's a catch, it's that tuition in London can be costly, especially for artists from overseas whose course fees usually top up those of their British counterparts. In disciplines that use elaborate equipment or materials, prices can be especially high. A term at the London Film School, for example, will set you back £6,400. That said, money spent on artistic tuition in this city is money well spent: make your mark here, and the dream of living from your art will become a distinctly more feasible proposition.

10

The emphasis in this chapter is on practical courses, those that enable the budding artist to become a working artist. London's academic courses devoted to the fine arts, performing arts, literature, film and modern media are legion, and many are excellent, but what we supply here are pointers to schools in the arts themselves. Study is good; getting your hands in the mix even better.

Most of London's better known artistic academies focus on aspects of a single discipline like the **Royal College of Art**, the **Rambert School of Ballet and Contemporary Dance** or the **Royal College of Music**. Other institutions have stakes in more than one territory. **Trinity Laban**, formed by a merger of the Laban Centre and Trinity College of Music, is the UK's first conservatory for dance and music, **Goldsmiths** offers courses in drama, music and visual arts, and **Birkbeck** (like Goldsmiths a part of the University of London) teaches acting, dance, writing, music and composition. Birkbeck is also London's only university to offer higher education through flexible evening classes.

An even larger arts complex is the **University of the Arts London**, whose umbrella covers the **Camberwell College of Arts**, **Central Saint Martins College of Art and Design**, **Chelsea College of Art and Design**, the

London College of Communication, the London College of Fashion and Wimbledon School of Art. All are modern, forward-looking schools with stimulatingly cosmopolitan corps of teachers and pupils.

Even so, a fair number of London's contemporary thinking schools also boast an aura of historic glory. The Metropolitan Film School is based at the famous Ealing Studios, the Royal College of Music occupies a lovely 19th century red brick building by Arthur Blomfield in the heart of affluent Kensington and Trinity College of Music is housed in the former Greenwich Hospital, a truly stupendous set of buildings designed in part by Christopher Wren on the model of Les Invalides in Paris.

Famous alumni add extra appeal; the Royal College of Music boasts Michael Tippett, Trevor Pinnock and Andrew Lloyd Webber. Sometimes it is the teachers themselves who are the luminaries. One of the best writing courses in the country is the MA in creative writing at the University of London's Royal Holloway College run by poet laureate Andrew Motion.

Artistic activity in London is also available in small measures. A short course at the Courtauld Institute of Art, say, or the Tate Modern Poetry Course, an

10

Curzon Mayfair
38 Curzon St, W1

eight-week course that draws inspiration from the art collection. Shorter still is the **Central London Writers and Poets of London**, a twice-monthly writers' workshop held in the Military History section of the giant Waterstone's bookshop on Gower Street.

Lights, camera, education

The **London Film School** is the oldest academy of film technique in the world, and one of the most respected. In the half-century since its foundation, thousands of filmmakers have passed through its doors, including excellent directors Michael Leigh and Michael Mann and celebrated directors of photography Tak Fujimoto and Roger Pratt.

Today the school teaches Master of Arts filmmaking and MA screenwriting courses, both of two-year duration. The schools philosophy reposes on three tenets: creative freedom, innovation and craft excellence. The LFS, housed in a converted warehouse, is organized along the lines of a working production company, with workshops, studios and screening rooms taking the place of traditional classrooms. Workloads are high: each student assists with at least one film in each 12-week term, which means the school produces more than 160 exercises and graduation films a year and many of those films then play at festivals worldwide.

As the London Film School website proclaims, nearly three quarters of its students come from overseas. The school's elegant Covent Garden location is just a short walk away from the West End's best cinemas and theatres.

10

Art, architecture & design

Camberwell College of Arts
Peckham Rd, SE5
⊖ Oval
ⓒ 020 7514 6302
camberwell.arts.ac.uk
⊕ Off map

Central St Martins College of Art and Design
Southampton Row, WC1
⊖ Holborn
ⓒ 020 7514 7022
csm.arts.ac.uk
⊕ 7/Q6

Chelsea College of Art & Design
16 John Islip St, SW1
⊖ Pimlico
ⓒ 020 7514 7751
chelsea.arts.ac.uk
⊕ 15/P16

Courtauld Institute of Art
Somerset House, Strand, WC2
⊖ Temple
ⓒ 020 7848 2777
courtauld.ac.uk
⊕ 11/Q10

Kingston College
Kingston Hall Rd, Kingston upon Thames
⊗ Kingston
ⓒ 020 8545 2151
kingston-college.ac.uk
⊕ Off map

Putney School of Art and Design
2 Oxford Rd, SW15
⊖ East Putney
ⓒ 020 87 88 9145
wandsworth.gov.uk/psad
⊕ Off map

Royal College of Art
Kensington Gore, SW7
⊖ Gloucester Rd
ⓒ 020 7590 4444
rca.ac.uk
⊕ 9-10/G12

Slade School of Fine Art
Gower St, WC1
⊖ Euston Square
ⓒ 020 7679 2313
ucl.ac.uk/slade
⊕ 3/O5

Wimbledon School of Art
Merton Hall Rd, SW19
⊖ Wimbledon
ⓒ 020 7514 9641
wimbledon.arts.ac.uk
⊕ Off map

What's on

Floodlight
floodlight.co.uk

Hot Courses
hotcourses.com

Study London
studylondon.ac.uk
timeout.com

Performing arts

Central School of Speech & Drama
Embassy Theatre, Eton Avenue, NW3
⊖ Swiss Cottage
ⓒ 020 7722 8183
cssd.ac.uk
✈ Off map

City University
Northampton Sq, EC1
⊖ Angel
ⓒ 020 7040 5060
city.ac.uk
✈ X4/U4

Circus Space
Coronet St, N1
⊖ Old St
ⓒ 020 7613 4141
thecircusspace.co.uk
✈ 4/Y4

Conservatoire for Dance & Drama
1-7 Woburn Walk, WC1
⊖ Euston
ⓒ 020 7387 5101
cdd.ac.uk
✈ 3/P4

Goldsmiths
New Cross, SE14
⊖ New Cross
ⓒ 020 7919 7171
goldsmiths.ac.uk
✈ Off map

Guildhall School of Music & Drama
Silk St, Barbican, EC2
⊖ Barbican
ⓒ 020 7628 2571
gsmd.ac.uk
✈ 8/W6

Laban Centre
Creekside, SE8
⊖ Cutty Sark
ⓒ 020 8691 8600
laban.org
✈ 3/P4

London Contemporary Dance School
16 Flaxman Terrace, WC1
⊖ Euston
ⓒ 020 7121 1111
theplace.org.uk
✈ 3/P4

Rambert School of Dance
St Margaret's Drive, Twickenham, TW1
⊖ Richmond
ⓒ 020 8892 9960
rambertschool.org.uk
✈ Off map

Royal Academy of Dramatic Art (RADA)
62-64 Gower St, WC1
⊖ Goodge St
ⓒ 020 7636 7076
rada.org
✈ 3/O5

Royal College of Music
Prince Consort Rd, SW7
⊖ Gloucester Rd
ⓒ 020 7589 3643
rcm.ac.uk
✈ 9-10/G13

Trinity Laban
Old Royal Naval College, SE10
⊖ Cutty Sark
ⓒ 020 8305 4444
tcm.ac.uk
✈ Off map

10

Film, video & photography

Goldsmiths
New Cross, SE14
⊖ New Cross
☎ 020 7919 7171
goldsmiths.ac.uk
⊕ Off map

London Film Academy
52a Walham Grove, SW6
⊖ Fulham Broadway
☎ 020 7386 7711
londonfilmacademy.com
⊕ Off map

London South Bank University
90 London Rd, SE1
⊖ Elephant & Castle
☎ 020 7815 7815
lsbu.ac.uk
⊕ 12/U13

London Academy of Media, Film & TV
1 Lancing St, NW1
⊖ Euston
☎ 020 8408 7158
media-courses.com
⊕ 3/P4

London Film School
24 Shelton St, WC2
⊖ Covent Garden
☎ 020 7836 9642
lifs.org.uk
⊕ 7/Q8

Metropolitan Film School
Ealing Studios, W5
⊖ Ealing Broadway
☎ 020 8280 9119
www.metfilmschool.co.uk
⊕ Off map

Fashion and design

Central St Martins College Art and Design
Southampton Row, WC1
⊖ Holborn
☎ 020 7514 7022
csm.arts.ac.uk
⊕ 7/Q6

Kingston College
Kingston Hall Rd,
Kingston upon Thames
⊖ Kingston
☎ 020 8546 2151
kingston-college.ac.uk
⊕ Off map

London College of Fashion
20 John Princes St, W1
⊖ Oxford Circus
☎ 020 7514 7500
fashion.arts.ac.uk
⊕ 6/M8

Istituto Marangoni
30 Fashion St, E1
⊖ Liverpool Street
☎ 020 7377 9347
istitutomarangoni.com
⊕ X8/Z7

London Centre for Fashion Studies
Bradley Close, White Lion St, N1
⊖ Angel
☎ 020 7713 1991
fashionstudies.com
⊕ 4/T3

West London College
Parliament House, 35 North Row, W1
⊖ Marble Arch
☎ 020 7491 1841
v-l-c.co.uk
⊕ 6/K9

Fiction writing and journalism

Birkbeck
Malet Street, WC1
⊖ Russell Square
© 020 7631 6000
bbk.ac.uk
⊕ 7/P6

Central London Writers and Poets of London
Waterstone's, 82 Gower St, WC1
⊖ Goodge St
© 020 7636 1577
⊕ 3/O5

London College of Communication
2 Elephant & Castle
© 020 7514 6500
lcc.arts.ac.uk
⊕ 12/U14

London School of Journalism
126 Shirland Rd, W9
Warwick Avenue
© 020 7432 8141
lsjournalism.com
⊕ 1-5/D5

Royal Holloway College
Egham Hill, Egham, Surrey, STW20
⇌ Egham
© 01784 434455
rhul.ac.uk
⊕ Off map

Tate Modern Poetry Course
Tate Modern, Bankside, SE1
⊖ Southwark
© 020 7788/ 8888
tate.org.uk
⊕ 8-12/V10

Multi-discipline

London Metropolitan University
31 Jewry St, EC3
⊖ Aldgate
© 020 7423 0000
londonmet.ac.uk
⊕ 8/Z9

University of the Arts London
65 Davies St, W1
⊖ Green Park
© 020 7514 6000
arts.ac.uk
⊕ 6/I.8

University of London
Senate House, Malet St, WC1
⊖ Russell Square
© 020 7862 8000
lon.ac.uk
⊕ 7/P6

10

See page 9 to scan the directory

SAATCHI GALLERY

INDEX

Page numbers in italics refer to chapter directories

11

11

11

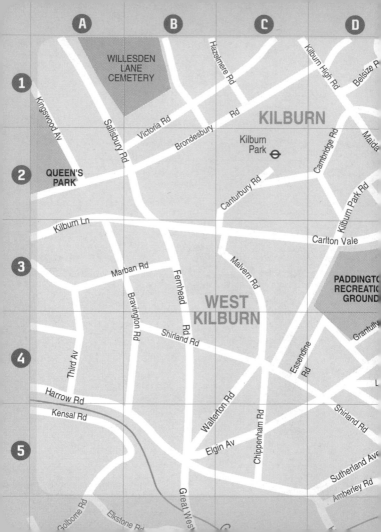

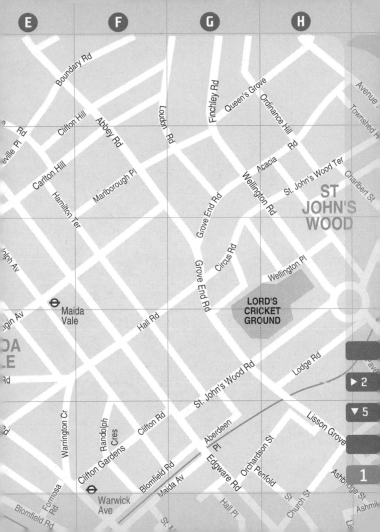

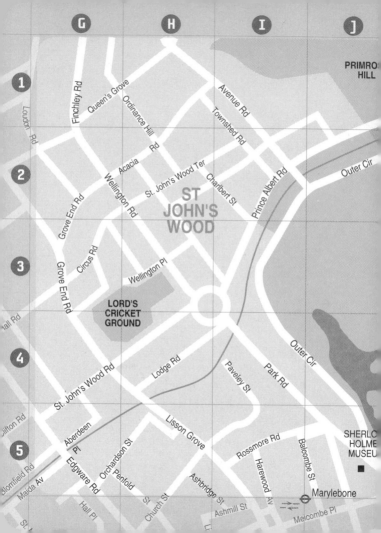

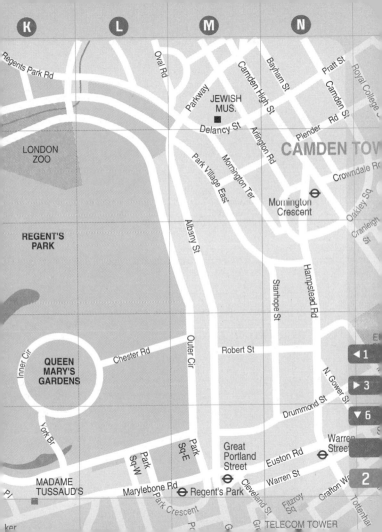

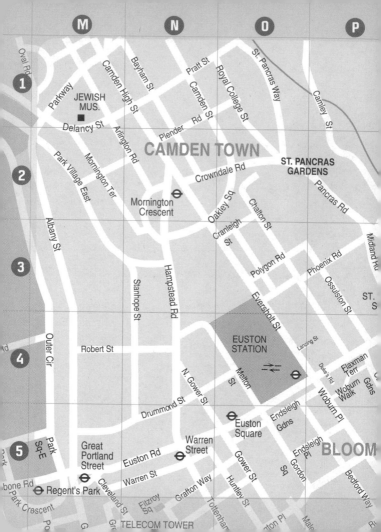

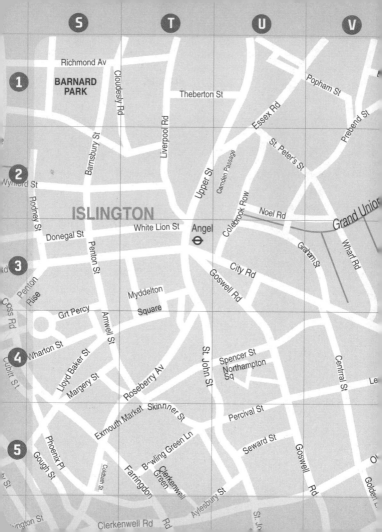

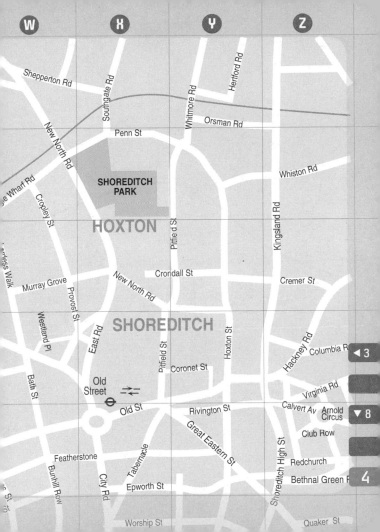

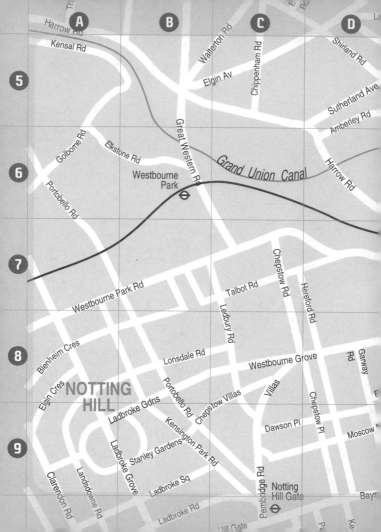

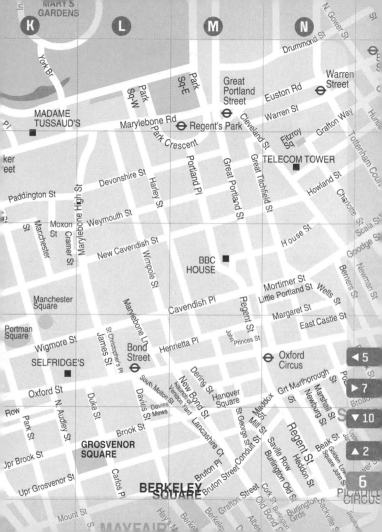

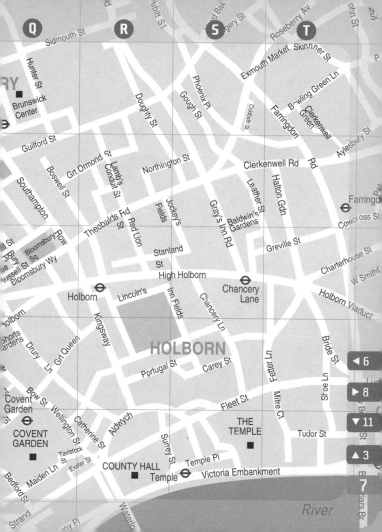

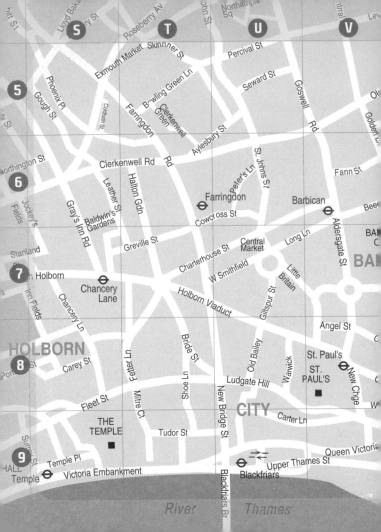

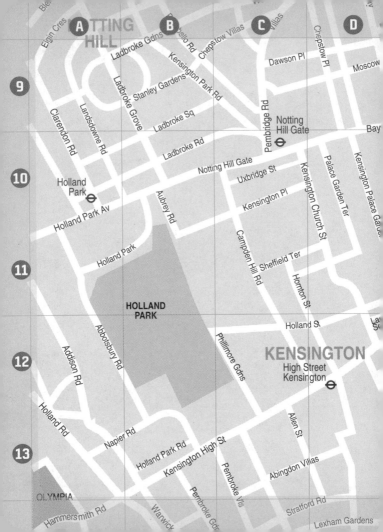

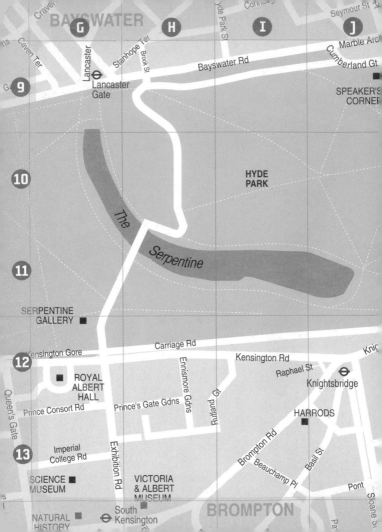

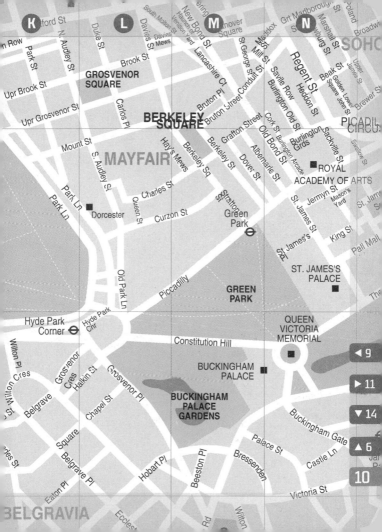

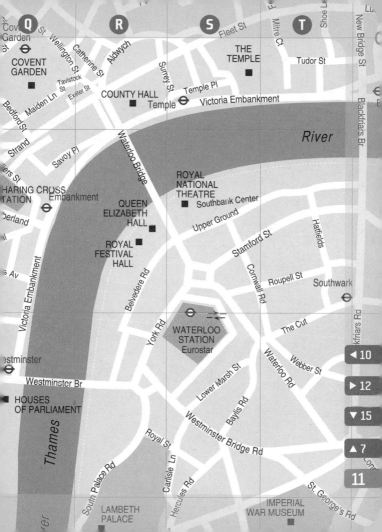

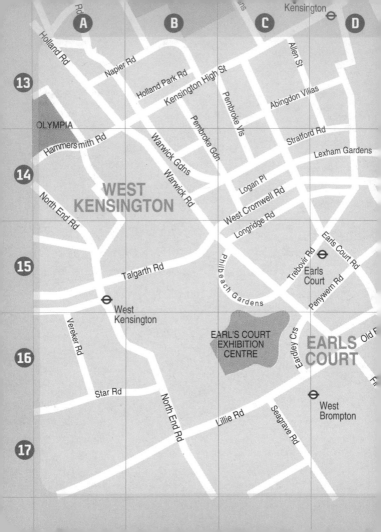

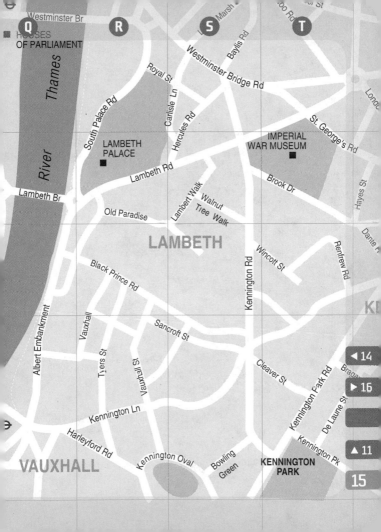

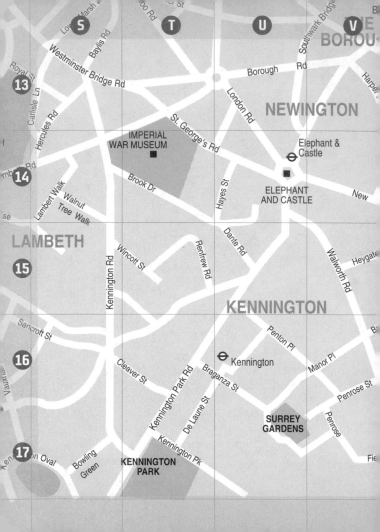

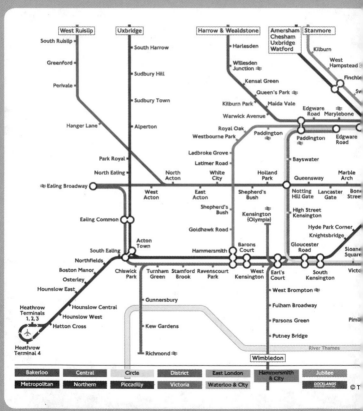

OTHER TITLES IN THE AUTHENTIK COLLECTION

Europe
Chic London
Gourmet London

Gourmet Paris
Chic Paris
Artistik Paris

FORTHCOMING AUTHENTIK GUIDES – SPRING 2008

North America
Gourmet New York
Chic New York
Artistik New York

Europe
Barcelona
Berlin
Milan
Prague

Asia
Beijing

FORTHCOMING WINE ROADBOOKS – AUTUMN 2008

France
Bordeaux
Burgundy
Champagne
Loire Valley

Italy
Tuscany

Spain
Rioja

North America
Napa Valley
Sonoma County

Visit www.authentikbooks.com
to find out more about **AUTHENTIK** ® titles

Simon Cropper

Simon is a British writer who has lived outside Britain for a third of his life; longer, if you count London as a country in its own right. Since moving to the capital some years ago, he's spent a commendable amount of time in its cultural power houses, sub-stations and fuse boxes. He writes widely on film, food and the arts, and is unshakeable in his conviction that Romy Schneider was the most beautiful actress of all time. Unless it was Donna Reed.

Alain Bouldouyre

Gentleman artist Alain Bouldouyre captures in his fine line drawings what our *Artistik London* author conjures up in words – the quintessence of the city. Art director for *Senso* magazine, and author/illustrator of numerous Art books and guides, Alain fast tracks around the world in hand-stitched loafers, a paintbox and sketch pad his most precious accessories.

K

COMMERCIAL LICENSING

Authentik illustrations, text and listings are available for commercial licensing at www.authentikartwork.com

ORIGINAL ARTWORK

All signed and numbered original illustrations by Alain Bouldouyre published in this book are available for sale. Original artwork by Alain Bouldouyre is delivered framed with a certificate of authenticity.

CUSTOM-MADE EDITIONS

Authentik books make perfect, exclusive gifts for personal or corporate purposes.

Special editions, including personalized covers, excerpts from existing titles and corporate imprints, can be custom produced.

All enquiries should be addressed to Wilfried LeCarpentier at wl@authentikbooks.com